HISTORIC PHOTOS OF
NEW ORLEANS JAZZ

TEXT AND CAPTIONS BY THOMAS L. MORGAN

TURNER
PUBLISHING COMPANY

In June of 1921, King Oliver's Creole Jazz Band opened at the Pergola Dancing Pavilion on Market Street in San Francisco. Pictured here from left to right are Minor "Ram" Hall (drums), Honoré Dutrey (trombone), King Oliver (cornet), Lil Hardin (piano), David Jones (sax), Johnny Dodds (clarinet), James Palao (violin), and Ed Garland (bass). Oliver's band proved to be quite popular on the West Coast, and his decision to return to Chicago was a difficult one to make.

HISTORIC PHOTOS OF
NEW ORLEANS JAZZ

Turner Publishing Company
200 4th Avenue North • Suite 950
Nashville, Tennessee 37219
(615) 255-2665

www.turnerpublishing.com

Historic Photos of New Orleans Jazz

Copyright © 2009 Turner Publishing Company

Library of Congress Control Number: 2009922658

ISBN: 978-1-59652-545-0

Printed in China

09 10 11 12 13 14 15 16—0 9 8 7 6 5 4 3 2 1

CONTENTS

Not much is known about Christen's Brass Band, a ten-piece band photographed at Southern Park, a tree-lined picnic area on Bayou St. John. The brass band was obviously a professional unit as shown by their uniforms, which have American Federation of Musicians patches on the collars. This first musicians' union was founded in 1896 to help provide members with loans, financial assistance during illness or extended unemployment, and death benefits.

ACKNOWLEDGMENTS

This volume, *Historic Photos of New Orleans Jazz,* is the result of the cooperation and efforts of many individuals, organizations, and corporations. It is with great thanks that we acknowledge the valuable contribution of the following for their generous support:

Library of Congress
Louisiana State Museum Jazz Collection

The author would also like to thank Hild Creed, Markus Sturm, David Roe, Leroy Jones, Eric L. Cager, Dan Marcus, Debby Davis, Erika Molleck Goldring, Dick Waterman, George Ingmire, Lars Edegran, Bob French, Lisa Kavanaugh, Preservation Hall, Olivia Greene, and WWOZ 90.7 FM for their valuable contributions and assistance in making this work possible.

With the exception of touching up imperfections that have accrued with the passage of time and cropping where necessary, no changes have been made to the photographs. The focus and clarity of many photographs is limited by the technology and the ability of the photographer at the time they were taken.

PREFACE

Anyone who has ever visited New Orleans would have to agree that it is a unique city. It developed with a myriad of cultural influences that in turn influenced the city's musical evolution. Being under the rule of the French and Spanish definitely contributed to a different environment than other cities living under British rule. The city's large slave population worshiped at Congo Square, creating an oral history of African culture and music. Religion did not disappear, music was kept alive, and dances were taught by those who remembered their African roots. For over a hundred years, New Orleans was the center of black culture in the United States when the prevailing opinion was that African Americans had no culture.

New Orleans has always been a remote area. Even with today's transportation, there's not another large city nearby that can be reached without many hours on the road. This isolation has both helped and hurt the city's musical development. Although it is one of the few, if only, cities that retains its musical identity, jazz music travels only so far north today. In fact, the city's rap music is much more influential to popular audiences than its jazz.

The pictures in this book are from one major source: the Louisiana State Museum's Jazz Collection. Though the archives are extensive, there are still many musicians from all eras of New Orleans jazz who are not included. Regrettably, there are not as many photographs documented here of musicians such as James Black, Alvin Batiste, and others that followed and played modern jazz in the city. Nevertheless, the pictures in this volume portray a vibrant jazz scene covering almost one hundred years.

This book organizes that 100-year span of music according to different eras in the New Orleans jazz scene, starting with the jazz forerunners of the 1890s and ending in the early twenty-first century with many well-known artists. Featured are some of the first bands including Buddy Bolden's band, whose leader is considered by some to be the first jazz bandleader, and the Original Dixieland Jazz Band, the first jazz band to record. Louis Armstrong, Edward "Kid" Ory, King Oliver, Oscar "Papa" Celistin and His Tuxedo Orchestra, Jelly Roll Morton, Warren "Baby" Dodds, and Sidney Bechet are just a few other big players followed in the book.

This volume has been a labor of love. There is no other city like New Orleans; there probably never will be. Hurricane Katrina made us all realize how important the music and culture of the city is and that it should never be taken for granted. Our music scene is as strong as ever, and there is a place for people interested in all types of jazz. The New Orleans Jazz National Park will soon open in its new home in Armstrong Park and will be a wonderful location for visitors and residents to continue their study of the unique music that New Orleans brought to the world: jazz. In the meantime, for both jazz connoisseurs and novices, the photographs here in *Historic Photos of New Orleans Jazz* bring to life the major players who shaped this spectacular Louisiana city and musical genre.

—*Thomas L. Morgan*

The Original New Orleans Jazz Band was photographed in Chicago between 1916 and 1917. They are, from left to right, John Phillips (Fisher) (clarinet), K. Fred Rose (piano), Merrit Brunies (cornet), Emile Christian (trombone), and Fred J. Williams (drums). This is one of the early Dixieland bands that recorded after the success of the Original Dixieland Jazz Band (ODJB). Fixed to the trombone is a strange mute, a device that changes the attached instrument's sound.

Way Down Yonder in New Orleans

(1890–1925)

New Orleans is the northernmost capital of the Caribbean and a major seaport. Because of its geographical location, the city has had a tendency to look south for its cultural influences rather than north. Culture and music were affected by the Haitian Revolution, which resulted in a significant Haitian population relocating to Louisiana. New Orleans had close ties with Mexico and Mexican culture; the Cotton Centennial Exposition in 1884 featured the Concert Band of the 8th Mexican Cavalry, which also played music of the Caribbean Islands as part of the program. The band continued to play for six months in the city. Later, the Tio family, who had spent time in Mexico, came in demand in New Orleans as clarinet teachers.

New Orleans, a unique Catholic city with its own costumes and customs, has always been known as a city that loved to dance. Thus, it quickly took to jazz and its precursors when they appeared. This music goes hand-in-hand with traditions such as Mardi Gras, a great part of what defines New Orleans culture. The Brass Band tradition and musical funerals, which seem to have German roots, also helped make New Orleans music unique.

This chapter explores the influence early New Orleans musicians had on the jazz scene. It also illuminates the differences between early art forms of jazz, such as Dixieland and black jazz, and looks at the families of jazz whose elders, fathers, and uncles taught interested young people what it took to blow a horn. The routes these eager musicians took to stardom started in vaudeville for some; others rode the train straight to the stage.

In particular, New Orleans music had an amazing impact on Chicago audiences, most of whom had never heard group improvisations by such virtuosos. However, this improvisational music was not a foreign concept once people heard it enough, especially after it was recorded. Musicians were bound to discover the secret language of improvisation—and when they did, jazz changed. Just listen to the difference in the Fletcher Henderson Orchestra before and after their exposure to the influential Louis Armstrong. Another one-of-a-kind, Sidney Bechet, inspired the first jazz review when a writer heard him play in Europe in 1918. New Orleans bands played jazz on riverboats up and down the Mississippi River for a number of years. By the mid-twenties, jazz was out of the bag and growing like a grass fire.

New Orleanians are looking to escape the summer heat in this 1892 view of Mannessier's Pavilion and West End Restaurant at West End, a resort area on Lake Pontchartrain that was popular from 1880 to around 1920. Many of the restaurants provided music for their patrons. The New Basin Canal ended at the lake, and folks rode trains or took the Shell Road to the site.

Various small suburbs such as West End, Spanish Fort, and Milneberg grew up alongside the lake as the city expanded from the Mississippi River towards the lake. These areas were popular during the summer heat because of the cool breezes coming off the lake. This 1892 photo shows some of the other buildings on West End, an area that was hit very hard by Hurricane Katrina in 2005.

Buddy Bolden's band in 1894 stands from left to right: Frank Lewis (clarinet), Willie Cornish (trombone), Buddy Bolden (cornet), and Jimmy Johnson (bass). Seated are Willie Warner (clarinet) and Brock Mumford (guitar). The legendary Charles "Buddy" Bolden was born in 1877 in New Orleans. He is sometimes credited as the first jazz bandleader, though the band's material was as much blues as pre-jazz. Bolden was known for his powerful horn playing.

This 1898 view of Canal Street, the city's major shopping area, faces Lake Pontchartrain. The photograph was taken from the Henry Clay Monument (not visible), which was removed from the foot of Canal Street in the 1980s by then-mayor Sydney Barthelemy. Canal Street was the original dividing line between the older French- and Spanish-built areas and newer areas of the city.

The Pickwick Club was the public face for the secret Mystic Krewe of Comus. Comus was the first Carnival krewe and helped form the modern Carnival tradition. Musicians were always a part of Mardi Gras and Carnival season, whether they were on the street parading between the floats or providing dance music for the lavish evening balls. The audience at the Pickwick Club would have been strictly male.

The areas along Carnival parade routes are always used in inventive ways to accommodate as many people as possible. The outside of this building facing Canal Street had bleachers precariously set up on the second floor for Mardi Gras watchers. Located on the corner of Baronne and Canal Street, this popular venue, the Chess, Checkers and Whist Club, was rebuilt from ruins after being destroyed by a fire a dozen years earlier.

Kid Ory and Band were photographed in Ory's hometown of LaPlace, sitting on chairs in a farm field. Seated from left to right are Ed Robinson (drums), Kid Ory (trombone), Lewis Matthews (cornet), Emile Bigard (violin), Stonewall Matthews (guitar), and Pops Foster (bass). Edward "Kid" Ory led one of the most successful bands in the city from 1912 to 1919 before he moved to California for health reasons. He performed at the 1971 New Orleans Jazz and Heritage Festival.

In 1909, 24-year-old cornetist George McCullum, Sr., joined the Barnum and Bailey Circus to play in the circus's band. He had marched in his first parade ten years before. After his stint with the circus, he worked in dance bands led by Joe Robichaux and Armand Piron. Later in the teens, he led bands in which both Manuel Manetta and "Sweet" Emma Barrett played piano. He passed away in November of 1920.

As a youngster of 12 years, Louis Armstrong got into trouble shooting a gun off on the Fourth of July. The incident landed him in the Colored Waif's Home, where Louis joined the brass band. He later acknowledged that he had played the cornet before being in the home but that he received most of his schooling at that establishment. Louis is pictured here (circled) in the middle of the front row.

The Tuxedo Jazz Band in 1914, from left to right, are Clarence Williams (piano, seated front row), Ernest "Ninesse" Trepagnier (drums), Armand J. Piron (violin), Tom Benton (banjo, vocals), Johnny St. Cyr (banjo, standing) Jimmie Noone (clarinet), unknown (trombone), Oscar "Papa" Celestin (leader, cornet), and unknown (bass). The band features some up-and-coming jazz stars, including Clarence Williams and Armand Piron, who would team up for future ventures the following year.

This 1915 picture shows Frank Christian's Ragtime Band performing in Milneberg at the open-air pavilion, Quarella's Pier. Christian was a well-respected cornetist who was in the Original New Orleans Jazz Band. The band featured here are (from left to right) Willie Guitar (bass), Manuel Gomez (guitar), Harry Nunez (violin), Alcide "Yellow" Nunez (clarinet), Frank Christian (cornet), Charles Christian (trombone), and Kid Totts Blaise (drums).

Fischer's Ragtime Band in 1915 consisted of (from left to right) Fred J. Williams (drums), George Barth (cornet), George "Happy" Schilling (trombone), Harry Shannon (cornet), Tony Barba (bass), and John Fischer (clarinet). The band retained the name even though clarinetist John Fischer had changed his name to John Henry Phillips, Sr. Phillips was one of the area's most well-known brass band and dance bandleaders. The picture was taken at Eastman Farm in Metairie.

Pictured in this 1915 novelty photo titled "Flying High in New Orleans" are three of Dixieland's bright young stars: clarinetist Alcide "Yellow" Nunez, trombonist Tom Brown, and cornetist Frank Christian. Brown would soon leave for Chicago, Christian would team up with pianist and comic Jimmy Durante in the New Orleans Jazz Band, and Nunez would join a group that became known as the Original Dixieland Jazz Band (ODJB).

Tom Brown's Band from Dixieland pose during a vaudeville routine at Lamb's Cafe, Chicago. The band, known as the Four or Five Rubes of Vaudeville, featured (left to right) an unidentified drummer, Tom Brown (trombone), Joe Frisco (dancer), Raymond Lopez (cornet), Larry Shields (clarinet), and Arnold Loyocano (piano). Costumes and vaudeville sketches changed with the 1915 show. Other pictures of the group feature the players with long coats and beards, while another shows Al Capone holding Tom Brown's trombone case.

In 1916, trumpeter Paul Mares, on the far right, was working with Leon Roppolo in Bucktown. Mares moved to Chicago in 1919 and was instrumental in putting together one of the most successful early jazz recording groups, the New Orleans Rhythm Kings. Mares was also co-composer of some of their famous songs, including "Farewell Blues," "Tin Roof Blues," and "Milneburg Joys."

That the civilian term for a sailor was a "jackie" explains the name of the West End Jazzin' Jackies, the 1918 U.S. Naval Station band in New Orleans. Posing from left to right are Paul Dedroit (trombone), Buster Klein (drums), Buck Banville (violin), Sal Castigliola (trumpet), John Bonnanati (clarinet), and R. Lane (piano). Paul Dedroit was the younger brother of bandleader Johnny Dedroit. Buster Klein later worked with Johnny Bayersdorffer, and Sal Castigliola joined a concert band.

The Original Dixieland Jazz Band, seated and playing in June of 1916, include Tony (Sbarbaro) Spargo (drums), Eddie "Daddy" Edwards (trombone), Nick LaRocca (cornet), Alcide "Yellow" Nunez (clarinet), and Henry Ragas (piano). The band would make jazz history the following year with their first release—the first jazz recording—"Livery Stable Blues." Yellow Nunez, who penned "Compliments Dixie Land Jazz Band" on the photo, left the band before they recorded.

A 1919 postcard was created in Alexandria, Louisiana, of Papa Jack Laine and His Reliance Band performing in an open-air theater. Laine had as many as six units working at the same time, all called the Reliance Band. Laine never recorded and left music soon after this picture was taken. The band consists of Jack Laine (drums), Charles Cordilla (clarinet), Alfred Laine (trumpet), Jules Riener (piano), George Brunies (trombone), and Herman Ragas (bass).

A picture from around the twenties of the Original Moonlight Serenaders features Arnaul Thomas (drums), Leo Dejan (trumpet), Harold "Duke" Dejan (sax, clarinet), Henry Casanane (sax), and Sidney Cates (banjo). The band was led by 15-year-old trumpeter Leo Dejan, but his older brother Harold was the best-known member of the group. Harold, who died in 2002, is remembered as the long-time leader of the Olympia Brass Band.

By 1919, the Original Dixieland Jazz Band (ODJB) had become world famous for their jazz recordings. In April 1919, they toured England for a year. Louis Armstrong always had a fondness for this band. He wrote, ". . . the first great jazz orchestra was formed in New Orleans by a cornet player named Dominick James LaRocca. . . . His orchestra had only five pieces but they were the hottest five pieces that had ever been known before."

In the mid-teens, clarinetist Israel Gorman worked in Storyville with accordionist Henry Peyton and Tom Brown's trio at Anderson's. He is wearing the band hat of the Camelia Orchestra and Brass Band, a group active from 1917 to 1922. In the mid-twenties, Gorman worked with Louis Dumaine, Chris Kelly, Buddy Petit, and Kid Rena. He was musically active throughout his life, recording with Kid Howard and George Guesnon shortly before his passing in 1965.

Freddie Keppard and "Big Eye" Louis Nelson (Delisle) were photographed in this garden scene. Both were well-known jazz men in New Orleans. Keppard was the next "King of the cornet" after Buddy Bolden. Nelson studied with the Tios, famous clarinet teachers at that time, and worked in the Imperial Orchestra in 1907 and the Superior Orchestra in 1910. In 1916, Nelson replaced George Bacquet to tour with Keppard in the Original Creole Orchestra in 1916.

By 1922, when the Original Dixieland Jazz Band's fame began to wane, the New Orleans Rhythm Kings stepped into the spotlight. Pictured are George Brunies (trombone), Paul Mares (leader, trumpet), Ben Pollack (drums), Leon Roppolo (clarinet), Mel Stizel (piano), Volly De Faut (clarinet, saxophone), Lew Black (banjo), and Steve Brown (bass, tuba). The band was popular for the next two years and made numerous recordings.

Alfred "Pantsy" Laine's Band, consisting of W. L. J. Cousin (drums), Eddie Cherie (sax), Sanford Mello (trombone), Alfred Laine (cornet), C. Cure (tuba), unknown (piano), and J. Treboquet (banjo), poses at Woodman of the World Hall during a WWL broadcast. "Baby," or "Pantsy," was the son of Papa Jack Laine, the earliest Dixieland bandleader. The younger Laine worked in his father's Reliance Band in 1908 before leading his own dance band for a number of years.

In 1915, Armand Piron and Clarence Williams started a publishing company. After touring briefly with W. C. Handy in 1917, Piron (far right) started an orchestra, pictured here at Tranchina's Restaurant in Spanish Fort in 1922. The band, which included notables such as Lorenzo Tio, Jr., (fifth from left) and Steve Lewis (at piano), played and recorded in New York City in 1923. Piron composed "Sister Kate" and "Kiss Me Sweet" during this time.

In 1922, when Joseph "King" Oliver returned to Chicago after a year's stay in California, his band was scheduled to perform at the newly redone Lincoln Gardens. Oliver, realizing that he needed to fortify the trumpet section in the group, sent for his protégé, Louis Armstrong, to join the band. Louis's addition changed jazz music forever as he took the first step to becoming the most well-known jazz musician in the world.

The Halfway House is one of few jazz landmarks still (barely) standing in New Orleans. It sits halfway between the city and Lake Pontchartrain on the bank of the New Basin Canal at City Park Avenue. The band in 1922 featured Charlie Cordilla (clarinet, sax), Milton "Mickey" Marcour (piano), Leon "Rap" Roppolo (sax, clarinet), Albert "Abbie" Brunies (leader, cornet), Bill Eastwood (banjo), Joe Loyacano (trombone), and Leo Adde (drums).

Fate Marable's Orchestra aboard the Strekfus Line flagship SS *Capitol* are Warren "Baby" Dodds (drums), William "Bebe" Ridgley (trombone), Joe Howard (cornet), Louis Armstrong (cornet), Fate Marable (piano), David Jones (mellophone), Johnny Dodds (clarinet), Johnny St. Cyr (banjo), and George "Pops" Foster (bass). Time spent in this band was beneficial for its musicians, especially Armstrong. Marable pushed his musicians to read music, and they spent hours rehearsing while traveling the Mississippi.

The New Orleans Owls are having some fun during a 1922 show at the Chess, Checkers and Whist Club on Canal Street. The Owls are Dick Mackie (trumpet), Eblen Rau (violin), Lester "Monk" Smith (tenor sax), Benjy White (clarinet, sax), Rene Gelpi (banjo), and Earl Crumb (drums). The Owls recorded 14 sides between 1925 and 1927 in four different sessions for Columbia. Three sessions were recorded in New Orleans and one in Atlanta.

A 1923 picture of the New Orleans Owls shows them in the Fountain Lounge of Hotel Grunewald, now known as the Roosevelt. Playing here are Lester "Monk" Smith (tenor sax), Earl Crumb (drums), Benjy White (clarinet and sax), Mose Ferrer (piano), Rene Gelpi (banjo), Eblen Rau (violin), and Dick Mackie (trumpet). The Owls were considered the best band in the South with the addition of 15-year-old Mackie, who described their material as "knocked-out barrelhouse jazz."

Around 1918, Clarence Williams left New Orleans for Chicago, where he set up a branch office of his New Orleans publishing company. In the early twenties, he moved to New York City and got involved in African-American blues and jazz recordings. For a time he was Bessie Smith's manager and wrote music for her early recordings. Sidney Bechet and Louis Armstrong both recorded with him in the early twenties.

The Tuxedo Jazz Band was photographed at the Canal Street Dock in 1923. The musicians are (seated) Henry Julian (sax), Sam "Bush" Hall (trumpet), Willard Thoumy (clarinet), Lawrence Marrero (banjo), John Marrero (banjo), (standing) Abbey "Chinee" Foster (drums), Milford Dolliole (drums), William "Bebe" Ridgley (trombone), unknown man, and unknown bass. "Tuxedo" is one of the long-lasting names for a New Orleans band.

King Oliver's Creole Jazz Band posed for this photograph in 1923. Louis Armstrong kneels in front playing the slide trumpet, then from left to right are Honoré Dutrey (trombone), Warren "Baby" Dodds (drums), King Oliver (cornet), Lil Hardin (piano), Bill Johnson (bass), and Johnny Dodds (clarinet). The band held court at the Lincoln Gardens, an integrated club that could hold over 1,000 dancers. The Creole Jazz Band recorded 40 titles for four different record companies.

As the caption says: Leon "Ropp" Roppolo hitting a few chords for the boys." Also pictured are Louis Prima's brother Leon, Peck Kelly, and an unknown "Don." Roppolo had a brilliant but short career. He was born in 1902, traveled in a vaudeville troupe at 14, and, in the early twenties, played with the Halfway House Orchestra before joining the New Orleans Rhythm Kings. He co-wrote "Tin Roof Blues" and "Farewell Blues."

Emmanuel Perez's Garden of Joy Orchestra played on the SS *Sidney* in 1925. Sitting are Alfred Williams (drums), Earl Humphrey (trombone), Eddie Cherie (baritone sax), Adolphe Alexander, Jr. (alto sax), and Caffrey Darensburg (banjo), and standing are Osceola Blanchard (piano), Emmanuel Perez (trumpet), and Jimmy Johnson (bass). Johnson was Buddy Bolden's original bassist. Perez, a cigar maker by trade, was considered one of the greatest parade cornetists in the city. He retired in the early thirties.

Monk Hazel, with Red Long's Orchestra, is seated at a banquet table in 1925. The musicians who can be identified on the right side of the table are Ellery Maser (sax), Monk Hazel (drums), Red Long (piano), Angelo Palmisano (guitar), and Joe Loyacano (sax). By this time, Monk Hazel was one of the best-known Dixieland drummers. He first recorded in 1927 with Johnny Hyman's Bayou Stompers, followed by sessions with the New Orleans Rhythm Kings and Tony Parenti.

Johnny Bayersdorffer's Orchestra in Spanish Fort is Charlie Hartman (trombone), Ray Bauduc (drums), Johnny Bayersdorffer (leader, trumpet), Joe Wolfe (piano), Hilton "Nappy" Lamare (banjo), Lester Bouchon (clarinet and sax), and Bill Kreager (clarinet). The club was the Tokio [sic] Gardens resort, described as a "palatial dance pavilion" with a 50-cent admission and special prizes for the best dancers. Bayersdorffer later took many members of this band on tour in California and Chicago.

New Orleanian Lizzie Miles was one of few blues singers who recorded in New Orleans and New York City. She left town at 14 to join the circus and spent eight years on the road doing minstrel shows, circuses, and vaudeville. Miles recorded the blues and popular numbers in the twenties. She had a career revival in the fifties on the West Coast, then returned home and released a number of recordings made there.

Jelly Roll Morton was the first important composer, pianist, arranger, and historian of early jazz. Morton said he invented jazz and that it was the "Spanish tinge" he added which made it so special. He played piano in Storyville, left town, and traveled all over the country. His 1915 composition "Jelly Roll Blues" is called by many the first jazz composition ever published. The late twenties recordings he arranged and composed are considered classics.

OH DIDN'T HE RAMBLE

(1926–1945)

It wasn't too long after King Oliver's seminal recordings that the jazz scene and jazz itself began to change. Jazz was popping up everywhere. Companies began to send out units to record in many of the United States' biggest cities, such as Dallas, Atlanta, St. Louis, Indianapolis, and even New Orleans.

Many people thought all New Orleans jazz musicians left in the late teens and early twenties, but there were still many jazz musicians in the city doing what they had always done: supplying the music for parades, burials, dances, and clubs. The music recorded in the city during this time shows that New Orleans jazz was going through a transition just like the rest of the country. Arrangements became tighter, improvised solos became more standard, and bands began to grow in size.

Jazz was becoming America's popular music, even though the Depression caused America's record companies to cut back on the number of recordings and which artists they chose to record. Despite the cutbacks, many radio broadcasts allowed jazz to be heard everywhere. New Orleans jazz musicians were spreading out, too. Duke Ellington's famous orchestra in New York featured New Orleans bassist Wellman Braud and clarinetist Barney Bigard. Cab Calloway's band had New Orleanian Danny Barker on banjo and guitar. A swing band led by transplanted New Orleanian Luis Russell was full of New Orleans musicians. Meanwhile, Louis Armstrong was making a name for himself as the "world's greatest trumpeter."

In the twenties, a second generation of New Orleans jazz musicians began to emerge, among them Louis Prima, Wingy Manone, George Lewis, and Sharkey Bonano. In the late thirties and early forties, there was also a renewed interest in the history of jazz. European music historians, then Americans, started to critique early jazz. Record companies began to reissue early jazz recordings. Jazz was here to stay—it wasn't a musical fad. It was America's music, and it went worldwide.

Oscar "Papa" Celestin's Original Tuxedo Jazz Orchestra, pictured in 1926, are "Wild" Bill Matthews (trombone), Guy Kelly (trumpet), Oscar "Papa" Celestin (leader, trumpet), Jeanette Kimball (piano), Narvin Kimball (banjo), Joe Thomas (vocalist), Abbey Foster (drums), Joe Rouzon (sax), Simon Marrero (tuba), and Clarence Hall (sax). The Tuxedo Jazz Orchestra recorded four times in the twenties for Columbia, resulting in 12 sides. Pianist Kimball was active in jazz for over 40 years.

Louis Prima's Band, possibly from 1927, are, from left to right, Irving Fazola (clarinet), John Miller (piano), Bob Jeffers (bass), George Hartman (trumpet), Louis Prima (trumpet), Cliff LeBlanc (trombone), Leonart Albersted (banjo), Jacob Sciambra (clarinet, sax), Burt Andrus (clarinet, sax), and John Vivano (drums). Prima, who became a major star in the forties and fifties, led a kids' band in 1923, then left New Orleans for New York in the early thirties and formed a new band there.

Louis Armstrong and His Stompers are pictured at the Sunset Café in 1927 in Chicago: Joe Walker, Tubby Hall, Louis Armstrong, Honoré Dutrey, Al Washington, Earl Hines, Bill Wilson, Boyd Atkins, Willard Hamby, Peter Briggs, and Arthur Bassett. Louis was beginning to make his mark on jazz with his recordings of the Hot Fives and Hot Sevens sessions. He also began singing, which proved to be as influential to jazz as his trumpet playing.

When trumpeter Ray Lopez (back-left) was 17, he joined Papa Jack Laine's Reliance Brass Band. In 1912, he moved to Chicago with Tom Brown's Band, touring vaudeville as the Five Rubes. In 1920, Lopez went to California and joined Abe Lyman's Orchestra. The band provided the music for the 1929 movie *Broadway Melody*, the first all-talking musical feature and the first sound film to win an Oscar for Best Picture.

Louis Armstrong's fame grew as he traveled around the country and overseas. Trumpet players young and old with something to prove would show up at Louis's gigs and challenge him to a showdown. Louis's then-wife, Lil Hardin, said he never lost a battle, but his whistling was what impressed her. Lil said that "Louis whistled even better than he played the trumpet." Regrettably, Armstrong never made a recording of his whistling.

In 1931, Louis (far-right with bat) came back from his touring quite a different man than when he left, but he was still the same old "little Louis" in many ways. Louis wanted to do something for New Orleans, so he sponsored a local semi-pro-baseball team, the Secret 9. Here is the team showing off the new "Armstrong" uniforms, caps, bats, gloves, and gear that Louis purchased for them.

Louis Armstrong visited New Orleans in 1931 for the first time since he left to join King Oliver. He wanted to visit the Waif's Home where he had been 20 years before. The director of the home, Captain Joseph Jones, and bandleader Peter Davis were still working there, and they posed with Louis for many pictures. Standing from left to right are Manuella Jones (Captain Jones's wife), Peter Davis, Louis, Captain Jones, Lil Armstrong, and Godfrey Moore (probation officer).

From June until August 1931, Louis Armstrong (center near microphone) broadcasted over WSMB Radio from the Suburban Gardens in Jefferson Parish. When the gig started, the radio announcer walked off the stage, refusing to introduce Louis to the segregated audience. Louis went to the microphone and introduced himself, the band, and the first number, quickly defusing what could have been a much uglier incident.

Armstrong's manager, Joe Glaser, kept trying to take advantage of Louis's popularity and turn him into a film star. Louis ended up appearing in both films and cartoons. This still from the short film *A Rhapsody in Black and Blue* is Armstrong's first film appearance. In a dream sequence, Louis, dressed in animal skins, becomes the "King of Jazzmania." He sings two numbers, "I'll Be Glad When You're Dead You Rascal You" and "Shine," and plays "Chinatown, My Chinatown."

In the 1938 film about horse racing, *Going Places,* Louis steals the show as Gabe, the Black Hostler. The highlight is Louis playing "Jeepers Creepers" on his horn to soothe the horse Jeepers Creepers, then singing it again, which spurs the horse on to victory. The song was nominated for an Academy Award.

A 1935 picture shows the Emergency Relief Administration Band in Jackson Square, which featured over 90 musicians in a federally financed project to help other musicians during the Depression. It was first led by Pinchback Touro and later by Louis Dumaine. Amazingly, most of the people in this photo have been fully identified. Some notables are Louis Dumaine, Sam Morgan, Cie Frazier, Kid Shots Madison, and Frankie Duson.

The Boswell Sisters, Vet (Helvettia), Connie, and Martha, pose at the piano. None of the sisters were born in New Orleans, but they spent their formative years in the city. At first, they played strictly instrumentals, with Connie on cello, sax, and guitar; Martha playing piano; and Vet with the violin, banjo, and guitar. The sisters' tight vocal harmonies, along with radio and film appearances, made them stars and paved the way for other vocal groups, including the Andrews Sisters.

A 1935 view of Luis Russell's Orchestra with their instruments arranged in front. Players standing in the front row are (left to right) Charlie Holmes, Paul Barbarin, Luis Russell, Louis Armstrong, unknown, and Albert Nicholas. In the back row are Otis Johnson, Pops Foster, Red Allen, Bill Johnson, and J. C. Higginbotham. Russell, an accomplished musician originally from Panama, won the lottery and moved his family to New Orleans in 1919. He led a big band for years and during this time was Armstrong's bandleader.

New Orleans–born Willie Bryant made his name in New York City as a bandleader and vocalist. He got his start on stage in the 1934 production of *Chocolate Revue,* and for a while he paired with Bessie Smith in the stage feature *Big Fat Ma and Skinny Pa.* In the mid-thirties, he led a big band while also working as a master of ceremonies, actor, and disc jockey. During World War II, he played many USO tours.

Trumpeter Sharkey Bonano and his band are pictured in 1938 at the Fountain Lounge. The band featured Doc Benitez (bass), Augie Schellang (drums), Sharkey Bonano (leader, trumpet), Clayton Durham (guitar), Freddie Newman (piano), and Nina Picone (clarinet). The Fountain Lounge was one of many venues inside the Roosevelt Hotel. The Roosevelt also hosted the Cave, which many considered the first nightclub in the United States.

In nineteenth-century New Orleans, observers in Congo Square heard the beat of bamboulas and the wail of banzas and saw the multitude of African dances that had survived over the years. The Square, located across Rampart Street on the back side of the French Quarter, was used as a gathering place for residents of New Orleans almost since the city was established. This is how it looked in 1939.

Along with Sidney Bechet and Jimmie Noone, Johnny Dodds was one of three important early clarinetists to come from the Crescent City. Dodds played in Fate Marable's riverboat bands before becoming an integral part of King Oliver's Creole Jazz Band. Dodds stayed in Chicago and recorded prolifically as a bandleader and an accompanist to blues performers. His most famous work may be as a sideman in Jelly Roll Morton's Red Hot Peppers sessions.

A studio picture was taken during Jelly Roll Morton's last RCA session in 1939. The musicians seen are, from left to right, Sidney Bechet (soprano sax), Sidney DeParis (trumpet), Zutty Singleton (drums), Albert Nicholas (clarinet), Jelly Roll Morton (piano), and Albert "Happy" Cauldwell (sax). Morton had been both composing and playing since the birth of jazz. His 1938 Library of Congress recordings still stand as an important oral history of early jazz in New Orleans.

Here is a 1939 picture of drummer Ray Bauduc. He was best known for his recordings with Bob Crosby and the Bobcats between 1935 and 1942. His early work in New Orleans included time spent in Johnny Bayersdorffer's band. Bauduc was greatly influenced by fellow New Orleans drummer Warren "Baby" Dodds. Bauduc and bassist Bob Haggart wrote the two biggest hits for the Bob Crosby Orchestra, "South Rampart Street Parade" and "Big Noise from Winnetka."

A 1940 picture captioned "All New Orleans Folks" shows musicians Arthur "Doc" Rando, Nappy Lamare, Eddie Miller, Ray Bauduc, and film actress Dorothy Lamour. Lamour was born Mary Leta Dorothy Slaton in 1910 in New Orleans. She won the 1931 Miss New Orleans beauty contest en route to Hollywood, where she was probably best known for her *Road* pictures with Bing Crosby and Bob Hope. Rando made a series of 45 recordings in the fifties.

When World War II was declared, many New Orleans musicians joined the service. This 1942 portrait features the saxophonists in the Algiers Naval Base Band. From the bottom up are Harold Dejan, Adolph Alexander, H. Trisch, Paul Barnes, William Casimir, and bandmaster Vernon B. Cooper. Paul Barnes and Harold Dejan are two of the better-known musicians pictured here. Paul "Polo" Barnes played with a number of well-known people, including Oscar "Papa" Celestin, King Oliver, and Jelly Roll Morton.

Algiers, sometimes known as the "Brooklyn of the South," is located on the south side of the Mississippi River but is still a part of New Orleans. It has always been home to active bands and musicians, including the Bocages, Henry "Red" Allen, Jr., and Sr., Memphis Minnie, and the Algiers Brass Band. Some Algiers venues included Philip Foto's Folly Theater, the Delcazal Playground, the St. John Masonic Temple, and the Ladies of Hope Benevolent Association Hall.

Jazz bassist Chink Abraham, better known as Chink Martin, is seen here along with drummer Monk Hazel and pianist Armand Hug in the forties. Though Hug was known primarily as a solo pianist in the Crescent City, he also played with Harry Shields in 1926, with the New Orleans Owls in 1928, and with Sharkey Bonano (with whom he made his first recordings) in 1936. Hug recorded up until 1976, a year before his death.

This is a 1944 picture of Louis Armstrong with drummer Big Sid Catlett and clarinetist Barney Bigard. New Orleans has always been home to great clarinet players. Bigard spent about 20 years with the Duke Ellington Orchestra before leaving to lead his own band. Some of the modern-day clarinetists who live and work in the city are Dr. Michael White, Tim Laughlin, Ben Schenck, Evan Christopher, and Louis Ford.

Warren "Baby" Dodds, brother of Johnny Dodds, was one of first great jazz drummers. He played in several bands in New Orleans before joining Fate Marable's riverboat band in 1918. In 1921, he joined King Oliver in San Francisco. After Oliver, Baby worked with Freddie Keppard and recorded a series of sides with King Oliver, Louis Armstrong, Jelly Roll Morton, and Johnny Dodds, his brother. In the forties, Dodds made the first solo drum recordings.

Playing in 1945 in New York City are Bunk Johnson (cornet), Alcide "Slow Drag" Pavageau (bass), George Lewis (clarinet), Warren "Baby" Dodds (drums), and Lawrence Marrero (banjo). In the revival period of New Orleans jazz (thirties and forties), many musicians got a second chance for fame if they lived long enough, like Johnson and Dodds. It also gave the younger and lesser-known musicians exposure to audiences in the United States and around the world.

"Big Eye" Louis Nelson, Pops Foster, Wille Santiago, Sidney Bechet, Albert Glenny, and Alphonse Picou are photographed in the Crescent City. Many of these important musicians had been around since the early days of jazz. Clarinetist Alphonse Picou will forever be known as creator of the celebrated chorus in the song "High Society." Picou, born in 1878, was given one of the biggest jazz funerals in New Orleans history when he passed during Mardi Gras in 1961.

BOURBON STREET PARADE

(1946–1960)

New Orleans in the late forties through the fifties mirrored changes that were happening nationwide. The music began to reflect the economy, which had decreased in size due to the length of World War II. Big bands of the thirties were pared down into smaller groups. The emergence of the jazz style Bop drew a dividing line for many listeners between old and new jazz. Bop not only divided listeners, it also divided dancers as jazz began to evolve from dance music into something to sit down and listen to. Many dancers moved on to the burgeoning rhythm and blues scene. New Orleans musicians were at the forefront of rhythm and blues and in the development of the Big Beat sound unique to the Crescent City.

New Orleans rode a crest of popularity as America looked back at the beginnings of jazz and realized that there were still some "original" jazz men alive and playing in the city. Bunk Johnson had a major career revival, and the city's Dixieland music scene thrived, especially on Bourbon Street in the French Quarter. Clubs were packed and new clubs opened. Jazz appreciation societies and new enclaves of traditional jazz lovers began to take root and grow.

A group of jazz enthusiasts began to put on their own concerts, which they often recorded. They began to collect mementos of jazz: pictures, instruments, posters—anything they could put their hands on. Called the New Orleans Jazz Club, they eventually opened the New Orleans Jazz Museum, where most of the photos in this volume have been taken from.

During this era, jazz began broadcasting weekly on local radio stations. The growth of television and regional broadcasts contributed to the growth of jazz, which continued to feed interest in the city's music and its musicians.

This is a still from the 1947 movie *New Orleans,* in which Louis Armstrong and his band were billed as the "Original New Orleans Ragtime Band" and Billie Holiday played a maid. It's a laughable story line but packed with excellent jazz and wonderful solos, including a duet with Louis and Billie. Their song, "The Blues are Brewin'," is a screen classic. The band, featuring Woody Herman, Kid Ory, and Meade Lux Lewis, was one-of-a-kind.

Radio broadcasts continued to bring New Orleans music to the region. This WSMB Radio broadcast from the Maison Blanche (ca. 1947) is composed of Johnny Wiggs (leader, cornet), Chink Martin (bass), Armand Hug (piano), Monk Hazel (drums), Boojie Centobie (clarinet), and Julian Laine (trombone). Most of the band members grew up in New Orleans playing its music, including Wiggs, who was born John Wigginton Hyman and recorded under that name in the twenties.

When Bunk Johnson was rediscovered during the jazz revival, he was considered possibly one of the greatest trumpeters of all time. Naturally, musicians wanted to find how they fared in cutting sessions and held this trumpet battle at the Twin Terrace Café in Chicago, featuring (from left to right) Doc Evans, Lee Collins, Jimmy McPartland, and Bunk Johnson. McPartland had been enthralled with New Orleans jazz since he was a youngster in the Austin High Gang.

Louis Armstrong proudly shows off his numerous Esquire Jazz Awards. In 1936, *Esquire* began giving jazz music awards that were initially determined by readers. In 1944, the awards were chosen by polling jazz critics and presented during a concert by the winners at the Metropolitan Opera House, a venue previously off-limits to jazz performers. In the 1944 polls, Louis not only won the award for Jazz Trumpeter but also for Top Male Singer.

Texas-born trombonist and vocalist Jack Teagarden always had a special relationship with Louis Armstrong. They turned Hoagy Carmichael's "Rockin' Chair" from a song into a comedy routine and back again. Their stage patter was legendary. Teagarden was one of a family of musicians with two brothers and a sister who were professional musicians.

Teagarden died in New Orleans after a performance in the French Quarter in 1964.

Playing at the Parisian Room in 1948 are Sharkey Bonano and His Kings of Dixieland: Roy Zimmerman (piano), Joe Loyacano (bass), Frank Federico (guitar), Sharkey Bonano (trumpet), Irving Fazola (clarinet), Monk Hazel (drums), Julian Laine (trombone), and Buglin' Sam Dekemel (bugle). Bonano was well known in New Orleans for his stage antics and trademark brown derby hat.

A 1948 shot captures Jack Teagarden, Paul Mares (center next to Armstrong), Louis Armstrong, and other visitors at a club. Mares, a friend from Louis's youth, went on to lead the New Orleans Rhythm Kings in Chicago. Louis always spoke fondly of the white jazz groups that were in the city when he grew up, especially the trumpeters. Mares retired from music in the early thirties but still performed occasionally into the forties.

WTPS, owned by the *New Orleans Times Picayune-States* newspapers, regularly featured New Orleans Jazz Club jam sessions live on the air. Pictured is clarinetist Irving Fazola and two unidentified musicians. It has been said that Fazola, born Irving Henry Prestopnik, was renamed for the musical scale (Fa-Sol-La) by Louis Prima, but further research shows that Fazola got the nickname from his childhood skill at solfège, a technique for teaching sight-singing.

Freddie King (drums) and Ruth Hardy (piano) attend a New Orleans Jazz Club meeting in the St. Charles Hotel. New Orleans has always been known for its strong drummers. Greats like Paul Barbarin, Warren "Baby" Dodds, and Zutty Singleton were the engines for many great bands. The city attracted drummers who wanted to play with the best. King, born in Decatur, Alabama, was active in New Orleans during the late forties and fifties.

Oscar "Papa" Celestin and His Tuxedo Orchestra had been active in the New Orleans scene since the early twenties. In 1949, he held court at equestrian Steve Valenti's Paddock Club, a Bourbon Street club with a horse-racing theme. This was the peak time for music on Bourbon Street, whose many clubs featured New Orleans jazz. The Famous Door and the Absinthe House were also popular establishments.

Bands have always been a large part of the Zulu Parade on Mardi Gras. The parade, which precedes Rex, starts early in the morning on Mardi Gras Day and winds its way through the neighborhoods until it reaches the main route on St. Charles Avenue. The best marching bands from the city's schools participate and are cheered for loudly, as are the numerous floats with riders throwing trinkets to the crowds.

Henry "Red" Allen's Brass Band of Algiers took part in the 1949 Zulu Mardi Gras Parade. For many years, brass bands and street music have been part of the city's celebrations, from parties to open up a new neighborhood store to political rallies. They parade to help raise funds for local churches and also to properly celebrate the sunset of one's life.

The African-American residents of New Orleans were excited when they received the first announcement that Louis Armstrong would be King Zulu for Mardi Gras in 1949. It was a unique chance for the black community to honor the city's most famous son. The tradition of the Zulus is to blacken their faces as their Carnival mask. This tradition is still practiced today in a predominantly black krewe, although some white members participate as well.

Freddie Kohlman and his band are pictured at Sid Davila's Mardi Gras Lounge, another great club on Bourbon Street where drummer Kohlman held court. The band features Frog Joseph (trombone), Sam Dutrey (clarinet), Thomas Jefferson (trumpet), Sid Davila (clarinet), Freddie Kohlman (drums), and Clement Tervalon (bass). Kohlman eventually left New Orleans in the sixties for Chicago, where he was the regular drummer at the Jazz Ltd. Club.

In a city known for its fine trumpeters, Sharkey Bonano and Oscar "Papa" Celestin were well known for their radio broadcasts and club appearances. A "Battle of the Bands" took place the night this picture was taken in 1950. Such battles took place to vie for bragging rights and to draw in crowds. They seldom resulted in extra money for the winner. This battle was broadcast regionally on WDSU Radio with announcer Roger Wolfe center-stage.

Louis Armstrong, Jack Teagarden, Barney Bigard, and Sid Catlett became the core of an early rendition of the All-Stars. From the late forties to early sixties, many musicians came in and out of this group. Not featured in the photo—but a longtime member of the All-Stars—was vocalist Velma Middleton, who also played the comic foil to Armstrong. The group toured extensively in this country and around the world.

This Bourbon Street establishment, Dixie's Bar of Music, also known as the Old Absinthe House, was built in 1806 and has been open as a drinking establishment for over a hundred years. It was home to jazz pianists such as Walter "Fats" Picon, Steve Lewis, and Burnell Santiago. Louis Armstrong was the attraction there during his 1955 trip to New Orleans. P. T. Barnum, Mark Twain, Franklin Roosevelt, Liza Minelli, and Frank Sinatra are just of a few of its visitors over the years.

Louis Armstrong and his All-Stars in 1951 are, from left to right, drummer Cozy Cole, trombonist Jack Teagarden, leader and trumpeter Louis Armstrong, bassist Arvell Shaw, clarinetist Barney Bigard, and pianist Earl "Fatha" Hines. Shaw was almost 20 years younger than the others. Hines was one of Louis's favorite piano players, and Cozy Cole was a well-respected and well-traveled drummer who had been a part of CBS Radio's first integrated orchestra.

Sidney Bechet (left) was probably as well known in Europe as he was in the United States. He first went to Europe in the late teens, then returned in the twenties and thirties. After World War II, he settled permanently in France, marrying a French woman in 1951. Bechet is shown here in Paris in 1952. He made his home in Antibes, where his statue was erected and a square named after him.

Louis Armstrong came back to New Orleans to play on a WDSU broadcast from the Municipal Auditorium. As Louis approached the middle part of his career, he stabilized his management by adding Joe Glaser as manager and soon became a recording star due to his lengthy contract with Decca. Next up for Louis was touring with the All-Stars. Pictured from left to right: Louis Armstrong (trumpet), Arvell Shaw (bass), and Barney Bigard (clarinet).

When Louis Armstrong brought his All-Stars to New Orleans in 1952, they had an impromptu meeting with the Basin Street Six, a newly formed Dixieland sextet with members including George Girard and Pete Fountain (third from left in front). Louis, always a gracious host, was happy to meet some of the old and young musicians from back home.

Paul Barbarin was important in the brass band tradition in New Orleans. Barbarin became the leader of the Onward Brass Band when his father, Isadore Barbarin, died. He organized it with the same instrumentation as his father had done, but with younger generation instruments. This modernization made the music more appealing to a new generation of brass band players and thus helped the tradition continue.

Myra Menville was a member of the New Orleans Jazz Club, which eventually started the New Orleans Jazz Museum. She was also publisher of the *Second Line* jazz magazine, the club's newsletter. She passed in 1979. Trumpeter Tony Almerico (at right) ran the Parisian Room on Royal Street and had a weekly coast-to-coast jazz radio show. The show, which eventually moved to local television, was a stop for Armstrong in the city in 1952.

New Orleans Jazz Club officials were photographed at a meeting in the Milton H. Latter Library, located in one of many opulent houses on St. Charles Avenue. Known as the grandest library in the state, it was built in 1907 and was a private residence to members of New Orleans high society. The Latter family donated it to the city as a library in memory of their son, who died in World War II.

Not many police departments can boast of their own Dixieland band. The New Orleans Dixieland Police Band is pictured here in 1952 performing at Audubon Park for the Home of Incurables. None of the musicians in the picture are identified. South Australia has a similarly named band that performs to this day, aptly called the South Australia Police Dixieland Band.

An early fifties shot of the Basin Street Six features Joe Rotis (trumpet), Pete Fountain (clarinet), George Girard (trumpet), Phil Zito (drums), Emile Christian (bass), Roy Zimmerman (piano), and an unidentified singer. The band was one of the first of a younger generation of Dixieland bands. They recorded for various record companies, including Mercury Records and 504 Records.

It is probable that
drummer Cozy Cole had
his picture taken with
two young New Orleans
musicians, George Girard
(left) and Pete Fountain
(right), when he was in
the city in the early fifties
with Louis Armstrong's
All-Stars. Girard was a
brilliant young trumpeter
in the Basin Street Six
with Fountain. Girard
had ambitions to take his
music nationwide, only
to succumb to cancer in
1957 at the age of 27.

In a 1952 publicity photo of the Three Coins and "the Fountain" at the Famous Door on Bourbon Street, the musicians are (from left to right) Monk Hazel (drums, mellophone), Phil Darols (bass), Roy Zimmerman (piano), and Pete Fountain (clarinet). Hazel was a busy drummer. Zimmerman was also a member of the Basin Street Six, as was Pete Fountain, who was just beginning a career that continues to this day.

In a 1953 picture of the George Lewis Band, Avery "Kid" Howard is playing trumpet in front on the left; Lewis is partially seen playing clarinet behind an unidentified trombonist. Howard played the drums with bands led by Chris Kelly and Isaiah Morgan. He also took to the streets with the Young Tuxedo Brass Band. During this time he was the regular trumpeter with George Lewis.

The 1954 funeral procession of Oscar "Papa" Celestin, trumpeter and bandleader for the Original Tuxedo Orchestra, is escorted by police. The Tuxedo name started in 1913 and had dozens of members under Celestin's leadership. After he died, the name was eventually taken over by his banjoist Albert French, also known as "Papa." When Albert French passed, the name was taken over by his son, Bob, who still uses it for his band today.

The Eureka Brass Band marches in a funeral procession in Algiers. These black-banded hats were worn in funerals, with the taller marching band hat called a "shako" and the normal New Orleans hat designated a captain's hat. The Eureka Brass Band has been active since the twenties and claimed many well-known members, including Percy and Earl Humphrey, George Lewis, Jim Robinson, and "Big Eye" Louis Nelson.

The Paul Barbarin Band in 1955 included Paul Barbarin (drums), Bob Thomas (trombone), Willie Humphrey (clarinet), Andrew Anderson (trumpet), Danny Barker (banjo), Ricard Alexis (bass), and Joe Robichaux (piano). Besides Barbarin, other band members who made their mark in jazz history were Willie Humphrey, who played with Jelly Roll Morton; Danny Barker, who spent years in Cab Calloway's band; and Joe Robichaux, who took a large swing band to New York in 1933.

Performing at the Famous Door are Abbie Brunies (drums), Jack Delaney (trombone), Chink Martin, Jr. (bass), Sharkey Bonano (trumpet), Harry Shields (clarinet), and Stanley Mendelson (piano). New Orleans has always been a place where older musicians play with and teach the young. Here, clarinetist Harry Shields is 37 years older than pianist Mendelson. At this venue, the band setup is located right behind the bar.

Closed in 1988 but reopened in 2009, the Blue Room in the Roosevelt Hotel hosted premier entertainers for more than 50 years. Leon Kelner and Castro Carazo were two of the venue's bandleaders. The Roosevelt Hotel was Huey Long's "home away from home" when he was governor. When he was due to arrive, Manuel Manetta's band was always engaged. The band would meet him at the railroad station and street parade over to the Roosevelt.

This is a portrait of NATO journalists at a New Orleans Jazz Club concert. The international group was interested in jazz music from New Orleans and how the Jazz Club was preserving and presenting it. Jazz was known around the world earlier than many people realize. Concerts were held in Russia in the twenties and in Singapore and India in the thirties. The first jazz review was of Sidney Bechet in 1918 in Switzerland.

Johnny Wiggs and His New Orleans Music, performing at the St. Charles Cocktail Lounge, are Sherwood Mangiapane (bass), Edmond Souchon (guitar), Johnny Wiggs (cornet), Harry Shields (clarinet), Tom Brown (trombone), Stanley Mendelson (piano) and Von Gammon (drums). Harry Shields and Tom Brown had been around since the beginnings of Dixieland jazz. Edmond "Doc" Souchon was also a member of the 6 and 7/8s String Band, an early New Orleans string band.

To sell his weekly radio gig at the Municipal Auditorium, Sharkey Bonano has taken his whole band out on the streets in a horse-drawn wagon. The entertainers Pork Chops and Kidney Stew are standing on the sidewalk. Band members on the wagon are Santo Pecora, Lester Bouchon, Chink Martin, Sharkey Bonano, Monk Hazel, Al Dorio, Jeff Riddick, and, holding a megaphone, WDSU's Roger Wolfe.

A highlight of Sharkey Bonano's weekly Sunday show at the Municipal Auditorium was the introduction of and interaction between Sharkey and the two dancers, Pork Chops and Kidney Stew. Here the duo, followed by Bonano and the clarinetist, are just finishing a second line out into the audience. Whether this occurred weekly is not known, but the audience certainly seems to be enjoying themselves.

One-armed trumpeter Joseph Matthews "Wingy" Manone played in the city as a young man. He began working around the country before settling down to record in Chicago and New York during the thirties and forties. Manone had many minor and a few major hits, mostly by reworking older material. Wingy, who lost his arm in a streetcar accident, was a good friend of Bing Crosby. His songs often provided a great sense of humor.

In the fifties, two brothers reunited in jazz at the Jazz Ltd. Club in Chicago. Pictured from left to right are Bill Reinhardt (clarinet), Munn Ware (trombone), Danny Alvin (drums), Sidney Bechet (soprano sax), Don Ewell (piano), and Leonard Bechet (trombone). Leonard Bechet, who was 20 years older than Sidney, was a dentist. He stayed active in the jazz scene in New Orleans, where he had his dental practice.

This postcard from the early fifties is of the Dukes and Duchess of Dixieland: Freddie Assunto (trombone), Bill Porter (bass), Betty Owens (vocalist), Roger Johnston (drums), Frank Assunto (trumpet), Artie Seelig (piano), and Mike Costa (clarinet). Betty Owens was married to Freddie Assunto and was with the group for a few years before she left to have children. His father, Papa Jac Assunto, joined the group as her replacement.

Active in show business for over 40 years, Louis Prima was well known for his music. He became even more popular when vocalist Keely Smith married him and joined his stage act. In 1966, Prima was the voice of King Louis, the orangutan in the award-winning Disney production of *The Jungle Book*. The film was nominated for an Oscar, and Louis received a gold album for the soundtrack recording.

The Kid Ory Band was photographed at the Hollywood club Beverly Cavern. Standing from left to right are Teddy Buckner (trumpet), Minor "Ram" Hall (drums), Joe Darensbourg (clarinet), Ed "Montudie" Garland (bass), Edward "Kid" Ory (trombone), and Harvey Brooks (piano). Ory rode the forties jazz revival to stardom. He recorded in the forties and fifties and had a band at Disneyland in the sixties. His tailgate style of trombone playing was a major influence on others.

Second line parades take place in New Orleans almost every Sunday afternoon from September to May. They follow a published route so that folks will know where to catch the band. Along the route are stops at neighboring watering holes and people's homes for refreshments. Here, historian and musician Bill Russell (left) is leaving the Caldonia Club on a second line staged for CBS-TV and jazz historian Fred Ramsey, Jr.

Drummer Sammy Penn, from Morgan City, Louisiana, moved to New Orleans at age 19. He found work with brass bands led by Chris Kelly and Kid Rena. Rena's interview with Heywood Broun started the jazz revival in the forties. Penn was also a member of the Eureka Brass Band. He toured a little, taking his group, Penn and His Five Pennies, to Chicago. In the fifties and sixties, he worked in Kid Thomas's Band.

Sharkey Bonano is donating one of his trumpets and his trademark brown derby at the New Orleans Jazz Museum. Behind him is a partial view of a jazz flow chart, showing its development and the various branches of styles created as it evolved. The New Orleans Jazz Museum boasted one of the greatest collections of jazz musicians' instruments in the United States. Up until 2005, the museum collection was housed in the U.S. Mint.

At the Sinton Hotel Concert in Cincinnati, Ohio, the Avery "Kid" Howard and George Lewis Band features (from left to right) Big Jim Robinson (trombone), Joe Robichaux (piano), Kid Howard (trumpet), Joe Watkins (drums), Slow Drag Pavageau (bass), and George Lewis (clarinet). Kid Howard, who could sometimes be found at the drums during his career, was widely recorded in the fifties and sixties. Howard was the regular trumpeter for George Lewis during this time.

Pianist and vocalist Walter "Fats" Pichon recorded with King Oliver, Henry "Red" Allen, and Luis Russell during the twenties and thirties. In 1929, he made a few blues recordings with Teddy Bunn and Spencer Williams. Pichon left New York City in the early forties to work the Mississippi riverboats, and in the late forties and early fifties, he had a regular gig playing piano and singing at the Old Absinthe House in New Orleans.

Ernie Cagnolatti (trumpet) and Sam Dutrey, Jr., (clarinet) appeared with Lawrence Marrero's Band in the late fifties. Cagnolatti worked with Oscar "Papa" Celestin, Paul Barbarin, and the Young Tuxedo Brass Band. Dutrey worked in various bands including Joe Robichaux's pre-swing band, which traveled to New York City in 1933 to record. These musicians were helped greatly by getting steady employment when Preservation Hall opened a couple of years later.

Preservation Hall has generated a renewed interest in New Orleans traditional jazz and serves as a mecca for those interested in mastering the music. Pictured here are Jim Robinson (trombone), "Kid" Thomas Valentine (trumpet), Orange Kellin (clarinet), and banjoist Charlie Hamilton. Kellin is originally from Sweden.

Pete Fountain, Jr., is posing with a group of women on Jazz Day, 1959. Pete, a founding member of the Basin Street Six, became well known from his performances on the *Lawrence Welk Show* in the fifties and Johnny Carson's *Tonight Show* in the sixties and seventies. In 1960, his club, the French Quarter Inn, became one of the hottest spots in New Orleans. He has recorded over 50 albums and still performs in the area.

One of the most famous New Orleans jazz clarinetists, Edmond Hall (right), came from a family of musicians. He had three brothers who were professional musicians. Hall played and recorded with many people in the thirties, including Claude Hopkins, Lucky Millinder, Red Allen, and Teddy Wilson. In the forties and fifties, he traveled with Louis Armstrong as a member of the All-Stars. He remained active and recorded until his passing in 1967.

This 1960 picture captures pianist Billie Pierce and guitarist Emanuel "Manny" Sayles at Tulane University. Sayles, who studied violin, also played banjo. He worked on the riverboats with Fate Marable and Armand Piron, and in 1929, he recorded in New Orleans with the Jones-Collins Astoria Hot Eight. In the forties, he led his own group in Chicago before returning to New Orleans, where he recorded and performed regularly at Preservation Hall.

The core of the Dukes of Dixieland was Fred, Papa Jac, and Frank Assunto. Reigning as one of the top Dixieland bands for 25 years, they were the first Dixieland band to record the Paul Barbarin classics "Bourbon Street Parade" and "Slide Frog Slide." Louis Armstrong was a great fan of the band and recorded many sides with them in the late fifties.

In 1960, the New Orleans neighborhood where Louis Armstrong grew up was torn down for urban renewal. One would have entered Armstrong's house, on the left, in Janes (James) Alley by going down the passageway between houses. The house would be an amazing tourist attraction if it had been saved. There are ongoing battles even today about preserving musicians' homes in the city. Houses where Jelly Roll Morton and Buddy Bolden lived still stand.

New Arrival

(1961–1975)

The 1960s brought great change to the New Orleans jazz scene. With the founding of Preservation Hall came a home for New Orleans traditional jazz that was different from any other club in the city. It gave aging musicians a chance to make a decent living through touring and record releases. As Preservation Hall bands began to tour, the world could see these musicians and hear them play. The musical experience left the world with new perceptions and expectations of New Orleans music.

Another change to the jazz scene was the opening of the Playboy Club in the French Quarter. Bandleader Al Beletto felt that in order to put together the best possible band for the club, it had to be integrated. Although for many years it had been illegal to have an integrated band on stage, the law was overturned, and integrated bands began to appear.

It cannot be overlooked that for many years in New Orleans, not all musicians were lovers of traditional jazz. For years leaders of jazz bands had come to New Orleans to enlist musicians to join their bands. In 1956, there was a modern jazz recording session by the American Jazz Quintet, which featured Alvin Batiste, Ellis Marsalis, Harold Battiste, Ed Blackwell, and others. But because only a few musicians in the city were interested in modern jazz, the recording was never publicized and was quickly forgotten. In 1962, however, things began to change. Nat and Cannonball Adderley came to the city to record, enlisting Ellis Marsalis, James Black, and Nat Perillat for a modern jazz recording. This, along with Harold Battiste's AFO label, gave African-Americans a new stake in jazz.

By the end of the sixties and beginning of the seventies, other factors in New Orleans began to change the jazz scene. Danny Barker's work teaching young people the business of jazz after years in the business himself, as well as his work with the next generation at Fairview Baptist Church, would have a large effect on music heard in the streets during the next 30 years. Then a little festival, the New Orleans Jazz Festival, was held in Congo Square, and it was only going to get bigger.

The original site of the New Orleans Jazz Museum was at 1017 Dumaine Street in the French Quarter. This picture of the 1961 opening ceremonies of the museum's dedication features some of the musicians who helped make the museum a reality. The band, Sharkey Bonano and the Kings of Dixieland, included Edmond Souchon (guitar and banjo), Emile Oulliber (trombone), Sharkey Bonano (trumpet), Monk Hazel (drums), Dan LeBlanc (bass), and Harry Shields (clarinet).

Carnival season always brings private parties and balls. Here is Sweet Emma Barrett and Her Jazz Band playing for the Krewe of Wrecks on Mardi Gras Day. The musicians are Josiah "Cie" Frazier (drums), Big Jim Robinson (trombone), Percy Humphrey (trumpet), George Guesnon (banjo), Ricard Alexis (bass), and Andrew Morgan (sax and clarinet). All these musicians recorded by themselves or with a group of Preservation Hall musicians during this time.

Leslie Milton learned drumming and showmanship from his uncle, Ernest "the Kid" Milton. By age 12, he was playing drums professionally in the French Quarter. In 1961, shortly after this picture was taken, Leslie moved to Los Angeles and enjoyed an active career drumming with Johnny Otis, Etta James, Ray Charles, Little Richard, and Ike and Tina Turner. He is now known as Leslie "Star Drums" Milton in Everett, Washington, where he lives and works.

Walden "Frog" Joseph (trombone), Joseph Robichaux (piano), and Andy Anderson (trumpet) are shown playing in Cincinnati. Joseph is father to sousaphone player Kirk Joseph and trombonist Charles Joseph. "Frog" was active in the New Orleans music scene not only in traditional jazz; he also recorded and toured with New Orleans bandleaders like Paul Barbarin, Louis Cottrell, and Papa French. In addition, he recorded with rhythm and blues artists such as Earl King, Smiley Lewis, and Dave Bartholomew.

George "Pops" Foster played with them all and outlived most, so when his autobiography came out in the late sixties, it debunked some myths and created new legends. He was in the Magnolia Orchestra and on the riverboat with Fate Marable, and he worked with King Oliver, Louis Keppard, and Kid Ory. In the thirties, he was a mainstay in Louis Armstrong's big band. He remained an active musician until he passed in 1969.

Clarinetist John Casimir was photographed in front of the Merry-Go-Round Club in 1961. For many years, Casimir was the leader and clarinetist for the Young Tuxedo Brass Band, who recorded for Atlantic Records in 1958. One number, "John Casimir's Whoopin' Blues," stands out as a harbinger of modern brass band music. Casimir played the B-flat clarinet with the jazz band, and with brass bands, the distinctively higher E-flat clarinet, an instrument rarely played by jazz musicians today.

During the fifties, singer, songwriter, trumpeter, and bandleader Dave Bartholomew was the New Orleans–based A&R man for Imperial Records, in charge of finding and recording artists, and—in the process—developing a sound that would change the soundscape of American music. Lee Allen, Earl Palmer, and Alvin "Red" Tyler were but a few of his sidemen. Dave recorded a large band jazz album in the early sixties that featured many jazz men from New Orleans.

Irving "Pinky" Vidacovich's Orchestra in the early sixties featured Tony Almerico, Frank Federico, Monk Hazel, and Armand Hug. Vidacovich (with clarinet, fourth from left) was also known as "Cajun Pete" in a popular local radio commercial. He performed with the New Orleans Owls, Princeton Revellers, and the Dawn Busters, the WWL Radio house band. In the late fifties, Vidacovich recorded with Armand Hug.

Trumpeter Punch Miller works with young clarinetist Tom "Tommy" Sancton. Sancton grew up in New Orleans, where his father took him to Preservation Hall for lessons. He was a correspondent and later Paris bureau chief for *Time Magazine.* One of many who learned their "chops" at the Hall, Sanction wrote a book about his experiences there called *A Song for My Fathers: A New Orleans Story in Black and White.*

Pianist "Sweet" Emma Barrett, known as the "Bell Gal" for the bells on her calves, was a self-taught pianist and singer who initially worked with the Original Tuxedo Orchestra under Papa Celestin. "Sweet" Emma became an iconic figure with the Preservation Hall Jazz Band in the sixties. In 1967, she suffered a stroke that paralyzed her left side, but she continued to work and occasionally record until her passing.

Dolly Adams (Douroux), born in New Orleans in 1904, was the niece of bandleader Manuel Manetta and the mother of bassists Jerry and Placide Adams. Musically, she was a triple threat, playing piano, bass, and drums. At 13, she played piano at Lulu White's Mahogany Hall. She worked with bands led by Peter Bocage and Alphonse Picou and led her own group that accompanied vaudeville acts at the Othello Theater.

Connee, considered by Ella Fitzgerald a major influence, was the most famous of the Boswell Sisters. After her sisters retired, she recorded for Decca. In the forties, she changed the spelling of her name from Connie to Connee, reputedly because it made it easier to sign autographs. Her duets with Bing Crosby were very popular; three of their records made it into the top 12 on Billboard. Pictured with her is Pete Fountain.

Henry "Red" Allen, Jr., was born in Algiers. He was involved in many groups, including his father's Allen Brass Band, before he left the city to join King Oliver in New York City. He worked and recorded with many people, including Louis Armstrong, Jelly Roll Morton, and Fletcher Henderson. He also actively toured with his own band and played festivals for the rest of his life. He is pictured with clarinetist George Lewis.

Dave "Fat Man" Williams was raised just outside the French Quarter. At five, Dave learned to play piano from his mother, an organist in the nearby Free Will Baptist Church. He worked in New Orleans after serving his country in World War II, but he didn't record until 1974. His composition "I Ate Up the Apple Tree" is a popular song in New Orleans and has been adopted by many brass bands over the years.

Jazz and blues vocalist Blanche Thomas is pictured here with clarinetist Louis Cottrell. Thomas began singing on Bourbon Street in 1944, then spent time performing in Chicago and Florida before returning home. She recorded for Dave Bartholomew and Imperial Records in the mid-fifties and at Dixieland Hall in the sixties. She stayed active in the jazz scene her whole life, eventually singing at Carnegie Hall in New York and appearing at Heritage Hall in New Orleans in the seventies.

Well-known jazz trumpeter Al "Jumbo" Hirt was born in 1922 in New Orleans. Hirt was classically trained as a trumpeter at the Cincinnati Conservatory (1940-43). Heavily influenced by the swing music of the times, he worked with a number of jazz groups, including those led by Tommy and Jimmy Dorsey. After returning home to New Orleans in the fifties, Hirt got involved in traditional jazz, sometimes working with Pete Fountain.

Banjo player and bandleader Albert "Papa" French was born in New Orleans in 1910. French was a sideman for Oscar "Papa" Celestin's Tuxedo Jazz Band for many years. After Celestin's death, French took over the band and became known as "Papa." The father of bassist George French and drummer Bob French, he made several recordings for the Nobility label in the early sixties.

A 1963 recording session of the Crawford-Ferguson Night Owls at Cosimo's Studio includes Paul Crawford (leader, trombone), Edmond Souchon (banjo, guitar), Jack Bachman (trumpet), Bill Humphries (banjo), Henry Kmen (clarinet), Sherwood Mangiapane (bass), and Leonard Ferguson (drums, co-leader). Kmen, an educator at Tulane University, wrote *Music in New Orleans: The Formative Years, 1791–1841,* the definitive book about early-nineteenth-century New Orleans music and culture. Cosimo's Studio was New Orleans' only recording studio for over 20 years.

Composer, educator, and pianist Ellis Marsalis, Jr., is pictured at top far-right with clarinetist Otis Bazoon and vocalist George French. Kneeling are trumpeter Teddy Riley and drummer and bandleader Bob French. Marsalis recorded in the early sixties with Ed Blackwell, Nat Perillat, and James Black. As an educator, he influenced a new generation of jazz musicians including Harry Connick, Jr., Terence Blanchard, Nicholas Payton, and sons Branford, Wynton, Delfeayo, and Jason.

Seen here in the Ernest "Punch" Miller Band at Tudor Arms in Cleveland are Noon Johnson (bazooka), Punch Miller (trumpet), Harrison Verrett (banjo), Andrew Jefferson (drums), Emmanuel Sayles (guitar), and Manuel Paul (clarinet and sax). Punch Miller had a long career working with Jelly Roll Morton, Freddie Keppard, and Tiny Parham. He moved back to New Orleans in 1956. Noon Johnson called his long homemade instrument a bazooka.

In 1965, the New Orleans Jazz Club arranged for Louis Armstrong to come back to his hometown. He visited the Jazz Club's museum and donated the trumpet he had used at the Waif's Home some 50 years before. Behind Louis is Peter Davis, Armstrong's band teacher during that time. He is holding Louis's horn. Armstrong would visit New Orleans one more time before he passed; the occasion was a 1968 pre-jazz-fest concert at Congo Square.

The house that Louis and Lucille bought in Queens in 1943 has been turned into a museum of all things Armstrong. Visitors can take a tour and hear audio clips from Louis's homemade tape recordings. They can also admire a display of Louis's adornment of acoustic tape boxes, which clearly show off his artistic side. A yearly concert series is presented in the garden of the house for the schoolchildren in Queens.

Although cornetist "Muggsy" Spanier was born in Chicago, he did play with King Oliver and Pops Foster. He always said that his life was saved at New Orleans' Touro Infirmary in 1938, and he wrote a song about it called "Relaxin' at the Touro." Here is Muggsy at far-rigst with New Orleans musicians (from left to right) Fess Hill, Art Johnson (tenor sax), Earl Robinson, Art Smith (drums), and Booker T. Washington (trumpet).

The recordings Louis Armstrong made in the last ten years of his life show his great interest in American music and musicians; they also show that he had no fear of revealing a new side of himself. During this time, he recorded Pharoah Sanders's "The Creator Has a Master Plan" and John Lennon's "Give Peace A Chance." Though his horn playing diminished due to ill health, his singing voice was strong, as proven by his recording of "Wonderful World."

This 1966 image shows two young boys playing with Paul Barbarin, who is on the left behind them. One of the strengths of New Orleans music is that musical families teach upcoming generations the ins-and-outs of the city's music. If they show an interest, these young musicians big enough to carry their axe are brought on stage or walk in the street at the next second line. This mentorship is a gift that cannot be measured.

Pictured here is Dede Pierce playing the trumpet and his wife Billie at the piano. The Pierces were jazz musicians best known for their work together. Billie was a boogie-woogie pianist and a blues shouter, and Dede was known for his songs in Creole. In 1935, they were the regular house band at Luthjens Dance Hall, where they stayed until the mid-fifties. They released recordings during this time which, in the early sixties, included performances from Preservation Hall.

This image shows Billie and Dede Pierce at Preservation Hall with drummer Josiah "Cie" Frazier. Frazier, a veteran of early dance bands, played with Armand Piron, John Robichaux, and "Papa" Celestin. He worked in the E.R.A. and W.P.A. bands during the Depression and played in many of the leading brass bands. Later in life, he worked and recorded with a number of people at Preservation Hall, including Emma Barrett and the Humphrey Brothers.

This picture is of three veteran jazz musicians: George "Pops" Foster, Johnny St. Cyr, and Earl "Fatha" Hines. Pianist Hines wasn't from New Orleans, but he made some memorable recordings with Louis Armstrong. Pops Foster revolutionized string bass playing and wrote *New Orleans Jazz Man*, a book that added much to jazz history. Guitarist Johnny St. Cyr worked with all the top names, including King Oliver, Jelly Roll Morton, and Louis Armstrong.

Billie and Dede Pierce are joined on stage by clarinetist Willie Humphrey and Alan Jaffe, owner of Preservation Hall. Jaffe also played tuba as does his son, Ben, the present owner of the Hall. At the time this image was recorded, Willie Humphrey was the oldest of that generation of Humphreys, which included his brother Percy. Willie, who primarily lived and played in New Orleans, was recorded numerous times and worked with Paul Barbarin and the Eureka Brass Band.

Another strong New Orleans clarinetist was Louis Cottrell, Jr. His father was considered one of the greatest early jazz drummers. Louis, Jr., studied with the Tios and Barney Bigard as a youngster then worked with many of the greats who stayed in the city, including Armand Piron, Joe Kelly, and Bebe Ridgley. He recorded under his own name in the early sixties and was president of the African-American chapter of the local musicians' union.

One of many bands led by Johnny Wiggs featured Wiggs (cornet), Frank Assunto, Sr. (trombone), Freddie King (drums), Doc Souchon (guitar), and Armand Hug (piano). Much of New Orleans' early history would have been lost if not for the collection of Edmond "Doc" Souchon. Souchon, a medical doctor, made a recording of songs he remembered from his youth. He authored *New Orleans Jazz: A Family Album* with Al Rose.

Jazz clarinetist George Lewis came to light during the forties jazz revival, though he had been playing in the city since 1917. Lewis recorded with Bunk Johnson and eventually took over Johnson's band after his short-lived reemergence. Lewis went on to become one of the most influential clarinetists in the traditional style. He toured Japan, recorded at Preservation Hall, and had a residency at the San Francisco Hangover Club in his celebrated elder years.

A performance at Preservation Hall features Jim Robinson (trombone), Alfred Williams (drums), Ernie Cagnolatti (trumpet), Alcide "Slow Drag" Pavageau (bass), Louis Cottrell (clarinet), and Emanuel Sayles (banjo). Preservation Hall withstood the test of time and looks very much like it did when this picture was taken in the late sixties. A touring group, composed of some of the best that play at the hall, travels around the world.

Percy Gaston Humphrey was born in 1905. The Humphreys were a family of well-known musicians over many generations: Humphrey's father was clarinetist Willie Eli Humphrey, and his older brothers were clarinetist Willie Humphrey and trombonist Earl Humphrey. Percy led his own group, "Percy Humphrey and His Crescent City Joymakers," and the Eureka Brass Band for over 30 years. He made many recordings, including some at Preservation Hall.

"Fats" Houston was the grand marshal for a number of brass bands. Here he is at his position with the Olympia Brass Band.
The grand marshal, who often wears a sash showing the band's name, sets the tone of the parade, whether it is a jazz funeral or a
normal parade. Since Houston's death there have been a number of grand marshals; one of them today is singer Wanda Rouzan.

Grand marshal "Fats" Houston is performing on stage in 1968 at Jackson Square. This concert was part of one of a few festivals that took place prior to the New Orleans Jazz and Heritage Festival, which was first held at Congo Square in 1970. It found a new home at the New Orleans Racetrack and Fairgrounds in the early 1970s. The festival has now been held for 40 years and has had great influence on the presentation of New Orleans and Louisiana music.

Booker T. Glass was considered one of the great brass band drummers. He was a student of Ed "Montudie" Gaspard and began his career with Holcamp's Carnival Shows. During his long career, he worked with the Camelia Brass Band, Wooden Joe Nicholas in the teens, and the Eureka Brass Band into the sixties. His son, Nowell, was also a drummer. Glass passed in New Orleans in 1981.

The funeral procession of Adolphe Alexander, Jr., is led by the Olympia Brass Band, composed of (from left to right) Alan Jaffe (tuba), two unknown trombonists and an unknown tuba player, PaPa Glass (snare drum), Andrew Jefferson (snare drum), Harold Dejan (alto saxophone), Manuel Paul (tenor saxophone), Booker T. Glass (bass drum), and Milton Batiste (trumpet). The funeral was held in front of the black musicians' union. "Tats" Alexander was musically active for over 30 years.

Paul Barbarin was one of the greatest drummers New Orleans produced. He worked with King Oliver and was Louis Armstrong's drummer for many years. Barbarin was widely recorded and composed two famous New Orleans songs, "Bourbon Street Parade" and "The Second Line." Both are still popular and played to this day. Barbarin died on February 17, 1969, as he led his band in a Mardi Gras parade the day after this picture was taken.

Guitarist and bassist Alcide "Slow Drag" Pavageau was known as "The Grand Marshall of the Second Line." In the forties, he played bass with Bunk Johnson. Here he is with other members of the George Lewis Band, another group with whom he spent a good bit of time. Pavageau was known to the national media due to his appearances at the head of parades. Why he was teaching the band anthropology may never be known.

Here is a view of Alcide "Slow Drag" Pavageau's jazz funeral held in January of 1969. The Olympia Brass Band is leading the procession. Musical funerals are not unique to New Orleans; long-lived pianist and composer Eubie Blake remembered seeing them in Baltimore in his youth. Anyone can have a jazz funeral in New Orleans— it just takes money to pay the band and a permit to parade on the street.

The important early Fairview Church Band posing in Congo Square are Raymond "Puppy" Johnson (snare drum), Derrick Cagnolatti (alto sax), Lucien Barbarin (snare drum), Harry Sterling (banner carrier), Ronald Evans (baritone horn), Stephen Parker (sousaphone), Charles Barbarin, Jr. (bass drum), Leroy Jones (trumpet), Morris Carmbs (trumpet), and Danny Barker (banjo), who founded the group. The first modern brass band, the Hurricane Brass Band, was formed by participants in the early Fairview Band.

Alan Jaffe (left) and Larry Borenstein were two important people in continuing the presentation of New Orleans traditional jazz. Borenstein, a jazz fan, hired local jazz men to play at his French Quarter art gallery to draw people in. The music there became so popular that he stopped showing art and turned it into a jazz club. Jaffe took over the fledgling club and turned it into Preservation Hall.

In front, "Tuba Fats" leads the Treme Brass Band. Both Tuba Fats and the Treme were important in the continuing revival and development of modern brass bands in the seventies and eighties. Tuba Fats was known for holding court at Jackson Square, where he taught up-and-coming musicians the nuances of working on the street. The Treme Brass Band, led by drummer Benny Jones, is one of few traditional brass bands left in the city.

Pictured here is the ceremony for Louis Armstrong in New Orleans after he passed on July 6, 1971. Then-President Richard Nixon said Louis was "one of the architects of an American art form, a free and independent spirit and an artist of worldwide fame." Louis said before his death, "I didn't wish for anything I couldn't get, and I got pretty near everything I wanted because I worked for it."

The Dixieland Band at the Heart Fund features, from left to right, Emma Barrett (piano), Louis Cottrell (clarinet), Harry Souchon, Ernie Cagnolatti (trumpet), Wardell Quezergue, and Jim Robinson (trombone). Wardell Quezergue led the Royal Dukes of Rhythm in the mid-fifties, which was influenced by Dizzy Gillespie. During the sixties he founded NOLA Records and emerged as the city's most gifted arranger. Musicians ranging from the Dixie Cups to Dr. John have made use of his talents.

The Crawford-Ferguson Night Owls are enjoying themselves at the French Quarter Festival. From left to right are Paul Crawford (trombone), Jack Bachman (trumpet), Albert Francis "Pud" Brown (clarinet), and Len Ferguson (drums). In the fifties, the Crawford-Ferguson Night Owls were a dance band for the steamer *President,* a popular excursion boat offering daily tours and nightly concerts. Leader Paul Crawford worked in the Tulane jazz archives and played occasionally with Punch Miller at Preservation Hall.

One of the highlights on Mardi Gras morning is the appearance of Pete Fountain's "Half-Fast Walking Club," originally known as "The Half-Assed Walking Club." The krewe, fueled by assorted beverages, is led by Fountain, with other musicians and their followers, on a route from Commander's Palace to St. Charles Avenue, then on to Canal Street and finally to Bourbon Street, where it ends at the New Orleans Riverfront Hilton in the early afternoon.

Jeanette Kimball enjoyed a 70-year career playing piano. Her ability to read music and improvise made her an in-demand musician in New Orleans. She joined and recorded with "Papa" Celestin's Tuxedo Orchestra in the mid-twenties and also met her first husband, banjoist Narvin Kimball, while in the band. She was with Celestin when he revived his band in the fifties, and stayed on when "Papa" French took over running the group.

Three musicians who made their mark on jazz in the city were Joseph "Cornbread" Thomas (clarinet), Alvin Alcorn (trumpet), and Eddie Pierson (trombone). Thomas and Pierson worked with "Papa" Celestin and then joined "Papa" French when he took over the band at Celestin's passing. Alcorn worked with Armand J. Piron, Paul Barbarin, and Octave Crosby. In later years, he played with Louis Cottrell, Jr.,'s Heritage Hall Jazz Band.

Edward "Montudie" Garland was an old-timer who played the string bass, tuba, and bass drum; initially, he was a member of Frankie Dusen's Eagle Band in 1910. Over time he worked with many bands, including Manuel Perez, Joseph Petit, Freddie Keppard, and King Oliver. In the early forties he worked with Kid Ory and eventually settled in Los Angeles, where he passed in 1980.

Bassist Placide Adams, son of Dolly Adams, was well known in the jazz scene for many years. In the fifties, he played for R&B stars such as Clyde McPhatter, Ruth Brown, Roy Brown, and Big Joe Turner. From the sixties on, he was active in jazz in the city, performing at Preservation Hall and working with Alvin Acorn in Commander's Palace Restaurant at the first of what became popular Sunday jazz brunches.

Jazz drummer Louis Barbarin, born in 1902 in New Orleans, was the younger brother of drummer Paul Barbarin. In the thirties, he worked the steamships on Lake Pontchartrain with Harold Dejan and Eddie Pierson. In the fifties, he worked with "Papa" Celestin and then with "Papa" French. He was a regular at Preservation Hall until he retired in the mid-eighties.

A 1973 view of the Onward Brass Band's rhythm section shows, from left to right, Louis Barbarin, Chester Jones, and Placide Adams. Adams led the Onward Brass Band in the seventies, but the band originally dates back to 1889. This image was first used in Jack V. Buerkle and Danny Barker's *Bourbon Street Black: The New Orleans Black Jazzman,* one of three books that Barker wrote about New Orleans jazz.

Trumpeter Milton Batiste was the leader of the Olympia Brass Band; he's shown here with a young Harry Connick, Jr. Connick is a well-known actor, singer, and pianist. His musical talents were developed at the New Orleans Center for Creative Arts under the tutelage of Ellis Marsalis and with pianist James Booker. He has been successful on stage, on screen, and with a popular band featuring many New Orleans musicians.

FEETS DON'T FAIL ME NOW

(1976–2000)

New Orleans jazz in the later part of the twentieth century continued to grow in spite of the city's geographical seclusion. The growth of funk music by New Orleans bands like the Meters and the Neville Brothers had an effect on the city's jazz. It was the music of the inner city, and as the next generation of brass bands like the Dirty Dozen, Rebirth, and New Birth began to take hold, the brass bands began to reflect the popularity of funk and incorporate it into their repertoires.

New Orleans jazz families continued to supply the scene with players of great virtuosity. Rhythm and blues and jazz musician Frog Joseph's son, Kirk, was the leading sousaphonist in the brass band scene. Ellis Marsalis's children Wynton, Branford, and, eventually, Jason and Delfeayo, added their talents to the local scene. Wynton and Branford have taken their skills to the national scene, resulting in even greater influence.

The continued growth of the New Orleans Jazz and Heritage Festival and the introduction of the French Quarter Festival cannot be underestimated in their effects on jazz. The festivals provided a professional platform for the world to come see New Orleans jazz in any form. The younger generation was so taken with contemporary jazz that there was some doubt as to who would be the future players at Preservation Hall. Jazz festivals grew worldwide, especially summer festivals in Europe. These invited many traditional and modern jazz men and women overseas and introduced them to jazz lovers around the world.

As the century closed, the jazz scene was as vibrant as ever. Clubs now catered to both modern and traditional jazz tastes. Musicians began to explore and add different world elements into their music. Jazz in New Orleans was still alive and ready for any visitor, whatever their taste.

After Louis Armstrong passed, it was determined that there should be a statue of him in New Orleans. The statue is one of the highlights during a visit to Louis Armstrong Park. This is only one of a growing number of statues honoring musicians in the city. A bust of Sidney Bechet is also in Armstrong Park, and in Legends Park on Bourbon Street, there are statues of Fats Domino, Al Hirt, and Pete Fountain.

Banjoist, guitarist, and author Danny Barker played rhythm guitar with some of the best bands of the swing era, including Cab Calloway, Lucky Millinder, and Benny Carter. Barker's most influential work came when he returned to his hometown of New Orleans. He put together his writings about early jazz and published them in three books. He was founder of the Fairview Baptist Church Marching Band and taught many young musicians about the music business.

Four brothers successfully brought their blend of funk, jazz, and soul to the United States and to the world. From left to right, the Neville Brothers are Charles, Art, Cyril, and Aaron. The Nevilles first recorded as brothers in 1978, although Art and Aaron recorded in the fifties and sixties, respectively. The Neville Brothers were perpetually the closing act at the annual New Orleans Jazz and Heritage Festival until Katrina; they regained this spot in 2009.

Drummer Alonzo Stewart plays one of the street venues during a mid-eighties French Quarter Festival. Stewart was the drummer with Kid Thomas Valentine. Kid Thomas was a trumpeter who had his own band since the early twenties, though most of his recordings are from the sixties. The French Quarter Festival has been held every year since 1983. It features at least three stages devoted to traditional jazz and offers seminars held concurrently on various early jazz subjects.

Nicholas Payton, son of bassist and sousaphonist Walter Payton, Jr., was playing professionally by age 12. A student of Ellis Marsalis at the New Orleans Center for Creative Arts, he released his first album in 1993. He is pictured here with long-lived trumpeter Doc Cheatham. In 1997, they received a Grammy Award (Best Instrumental Solo) for the album *Doc Cheatham & Nicholas Payton*.

Wynton and Branford Marsalis blow at the 1984 New Orleans' World Fair. Both sons of Ellis Marsalis have been highly successful as musicians. Eldest son Branford worked with Art Blakely and Lionel Hampton, and he led the *Tonight Show* orchestra in the nineties. Wynton is adept at both classical and jazz music. He is the artistic director of Jazz at Lincoln Center and has won the Pulitzer Prize for Music for *Blood on the Fields.*

Danny and Blue Lu Barker pose for this photograph at their home in 1987. Blues and jazz singer Blue Lu Barker came to prominence in the thirties with sassy blues like "Don't You Feel My Leg," often with husband Danny Barker leading the band and contributing songs. Billie Holiday considered Blue Lu a great influence on her singing style. Blue Lu Barker was inducted into the Louisiana Blues Hall of Fame in 1997.

The Dirty Dozen Brass Band's roots are in the youth music program at New Orleans' Fairview Baptist Church. The church band eventually formed the Hurricane Brass Band, which led to the formation of the Tornado Brass Band. In 1977, drummer Benny Jones started the Dirty Dozen Brass Band, the first of the modern brass bands. Their success has spawned a new generation of modern brass bands.

Pictured here is the Original New Orleans Buck Jumpers' second line at the 1987 New Orleans Jazz and Heritage Festival. The Buck Jumpers are one of many Social Aid and Pleasure Clubs (SA & PC) that grew out of lack of burial insurance coverage for people of color in the 1800s. As times changed, the groups became involved in contributing to other worthy causes. Today, each club celebrates by dressing up and dancing in the streets to a brass band.

The New Orleans Ragtime Orchestra includes Paul Crawford (trombone), Bill Russell (violin), John Robichaux (drum), Walter Payton, Jr. (bass), Lionel Ferbos (trumpet), Orange Kellin (clarinet), and Lars Edegran (leader, piano). The group, patterned after the 1960 Love-Jiles Ragtime Orchestra, successfully presented ragtime in an orchestral setting. Over the years, the band has changed members on their numerous recordings but are still in great demand.

New Orleans–born vocalist Germaine Bazzle is probably scatting at one of her many appearances at the New Orleans Jazz and Heritage Festival. Bazzle was a music major at Xavier University and taught singing for years in the city. She is a member of the New World Ensemble, an all-black choral group, and has been performing in local nightclubs for the past 40 years. Despite being one of the best female vocalists in the city, she has rarely recorded.

Pud Brown (clarinet) and Lionel Ferbos (trumpet) wail at the 1993 New Orleans Jazz and Heritage Festival. At the time of this writing, 98-year-old Lionel Ferbos was the oldest active jazz musician in New Orleans. In the mid-sixties, he joined the New Orleans Ragtime Orchestra and is still a member. For many years, he has led his own group, which plays weekly at the Palm Court, a restaurant and venue for jazz performances.

Educator and saxophonist Donald Harrison, Jr., is the son of Mardi Gras Indian Chief Donald Harrison, Sr. The younger Harrison honed his skills at 21 with Art Blakey's Jazz Messengers. "The King of Nouveau Swing" has recorded many albums over the years, including the 1991 standout *Indian Blues,* a jazz tribute to the Mardi Gras Indian music of New Orleans. Harrison is the Big Chief of Congo Square with his gang The Congo Nation.

Composer, producer, and pianist Allen Toussaint's first recording project was *Wild Sound of New Orleans.* He was then hired by Minit Records. It was for Minit that Toussaint's songwriting and producing abilities were honed and begin to shine. Toussaint eventually formed his own series of labels with Marshall Sehorn; in the early seventies they created Sea-Saint Studios. Allen's most recent work, *The Bright Mississippi,* shows his interest and love for New Orleans traditional jazz.

Bassist for the longstanding modern jazz group Astral Project, James Singleton shows off his skills on the trumpet at a New Orleans Jazz and Heritage Festival appearance. Other members of Astral Project not pictured are Tony Dagradi (sax), Steve Masakowski (guitar), and Johnny Vidacovich (drums). Singleton has many musical side projects, as do others of the group. He leads and has recorded two albums with the avant-garde group 3 Now 4.

Vocalist Banu Gibson includes many songs from the thirties and forties in her repertoire. Raised in Hollywood, Florida, Banu studied dance from the age of three and voice from the age of nine. She has performed all over the world, touring Europe with cornetist Wild Bill Davison and taking her group New Orleans Hot Jazz to venues in Germany, England, Sweden, and Australia. She has recently worked on a CD songbook of Johnny Mercer compositions.

Composer, arranger, performer, and teacher Harold Battiste was born in 1931 in New Orleans. Battiste worked for Specialty Records in the fifties as an arranger and sideman. In 1961, he founded the first African-American–musician-owned record label, AFO (All For One) Records. It was Battiste who introduced Mac Rebennack as "Dr. John" and produced his earliest albums. Battiste is still actively recording, serving on numerous boards, and teaching.

Saxophonist and educator Kidd Jordan has an impressive list of people with whom he has worked, including Stevie Wonder, Professor Longhair, Sun Ra, Ray Charles, Ornette Coleman, and Cannonball Adderley. He had a long tenure as a music teacher at Southern University and continues to work with young musicians at the Satchmo Summer Camp. He is the father of jazz trumpeter Marlon Jordan and jazz vocalist Stephanie Jordan.

Trumpeter, vocalist, and entertainer Kermit Ruffins started playing trumpet in eighth grade at Lawless Junior High School in the Ninth Ward of New Orleans. In 1983, he cofounded the Rebirth Brass Band, with whom he toured and recorded for about nine years before putting together his own group, The Barbecue Swingers, in 1992. Heavily influenced by Louis Armstrong, Kermit is one of the strongest trumpeters in the city and certainly the city's best-known entertainer.

Notes on the Photographs

These notes, listed by page number, attempt to include all aspects known of the photographs. Each of the photographs is identified by the page number, photograph's title or description, photographer and collection, archive, and call or box number when applicable. Although every attempt was made to collect available data, in some cases complete data was unavailable due to the age and condition of some of the photographs and records.

63 **"Brooklyn of the South" Bands**
Louisiana State Museum Jazz Collection
1978.118(B).07783

64 **Chink Martin, Monk Hazel, and Armand Hug**
Louisiana State Museum Jazz Collection
1978.118(B).04851

65 **Louis, Big Sid Catlett, and Barney Bigard**
Louisiana State Museum Jazz Collection
1978.118(B).00208

66 **Warren "Baby" Dodds at Drums**
Louisiana State Museum Jazz Collection
1978.118(B).02675

67 **Johnson, Pavageau, Lewis, Dodds, and Marrero**
Louisiana State Museum Jazz Collection
1978.118(B).04162

68 **Nelson, Foster, Santiago, Bechet, Glenny, and Picou**
Louisiana State Museum Jazz Collection
1978.118(B).03121

70 **Louis Armstrong and Billie Holiday in "New Orleans"**
Louisiana State Museum Jazz Collection
1978.118(B).00941

71 **WSMB Radio Broadcast with Johnny Wiggs**
Louisiana State Museum Jazz Collection
1978.118(B).07021

72 **Trumpet Battle with Bunk Johnson**
Louisiana State Museum Jazz Collection
1978.118(B).04167

73 **Louis Armstrong with Esquire Awards**
Louisiana State Museum Jazz Collection
1978.118(B).00927

74 **Jack Teagarden**
Louisiana State Museum Jazz Collection
1978.118(B).06718

75 **Sharkey Bonano and His Kings of Dixieland at the Parisian Room**
Louisiana State Museum Jazz Collection
1978.118(B).00797

76 **Teagarden, Mares, and Armstrong**
Louisiana State Museum Jazz Collection
1978.118(B).04786

77 **Irving Fazola and WTPS Trio**
Louisiana State Museum Jazz Collection
1995.111.2

78 **Freddie King and Ruth Hardy with New Orleans Jazz Club**
Louisiana State Museum Jazz Collection
1978.118(B).04292

79 **Tuxedo Orchestra at the Paddock Club**
Louisiana State Museum Jazz Collection
1978.118(B).02179

80 **Band Marching in the Zulu Parade**
Louisiana State Museum Jazz Collection
1978.118(B).07303b

81 **"Red" Allen's Brass Band of Algiers in Zulu Parade**
Louisiana State Museum Jazz Collection
1978.118(B).07303g

82 **Louis as King Zulu**
Louisiana State Museum Jazz Collection
1978.118(B).07300i

83 **Freddie Kohlman and Band at Sid DaVilla's**
Louisiana State Museum Jazz Collection
1989.141.2

84 **Battle of the Bands**
Louisiana State Museum Jazz Collection
1978.118(B).02192

85 **Early Rendition of the All-Stars**
Louisiana State Museum Jazz Collection
1978.118(B).00921

86 **Dixie's Bar of Music**
Library of Congress
073038pu

87 **Louis and his All-Stars, 1951**
Louisiana State Museum Jazz Collection
1978.118(B).07276

88 **Bechet in Paris, 1952**
Louisiana State Museum Jazz Collection
1978.118(B).00571

89 **Louis Broadcasting from the Municipal Auditorium**
Louisiana State Museum Jazz Collection
1978.118(B).00922

90 **The All-Stars Meet the Basin Street Six**
Louisiana State Museum Jazz Collection
1978.118(B).0918

91 **Paul Barbarin**
Louisiana State Museum Jazz Collection
1978.118(B).0315

92 **Myra Menville and the New Orleans Jazz Club**
Louisiana State Museum Jazz Collection
1978.118(B).0917

93 **New Orleans Jazz Club at the Milton H. Latter Library**
Louisiana State Museum Jazz Collection
1978.118(B).05351

94 **The New Orleans Dixieland Police Band**
Louisiana State Museum Jazz Collection
1978.118(B).05402

95 **The Basin Street Six**
Louisiana State Museum Jazz Collection
1978.118(B).03131

96 **Cozy Cole Posing with Musicians**
Louisiana State Museum Jazz Collection
1978.118(B).03138

97 **The Three Coins and "The Fountain"**
Louisiana State Museum Jazz Collection
1978.118(B).03149

98 **George Lewis Band with Avery "Kid" Howard**
Louisiana State Museum Jazz Collection
1978.118(B).03789

99 **Funeral Procession of Oscar Celestin**
Louisiana State Museum Jazz Collection
1978.118(B).02199

100 THE EUREKA BRASS BAND
Louisiana State Museum Jazz Collection
1978.118(B).02938

101 THE PAUL BARBARIN BAND, 1955
Louisiana State Museum Jazz Collection
1978.118(B).07784

102 BAND PERFORMING AT THE FAMOUS DOOR
Louisiana State Museum Jazz Collection
1978.118(B).00787

103 THE BLUE ROOM IN THE ROOSEVELT HOTEL
Louisiana State Museum Jazz Collection
1978.118(B).0837

104 NATO JOURNALISTS AT A NEW ORLEANS JAZZ CLUB CONCERT
Louisiana State Museum Jazz Collection
1978.118(B).05268

105 JOHNNY WIGGS AND HIS NEW ORLEANS MUSIC
Louisiana State Museum Jazz Collection
1978.118(B).04726

106 BONANO AND BAND IN HORSE-DRAWN WAGON
Louisiana State Museum Jazz Collection
1978.118(B).0832a

107 PORK CHOPS AND KIDNEY STEW PERFORMING ON BONANO'S SHOW
Louisiana State Museum Jazz Collection
1978.118(B).00780

108 JOSEPH MATTHEWS "WINGY" MANONE
Louisiana State Museum Jazz Collection
1978.118(B).00175

109 BROTHERS REUNITING AT THE JAZZ LTD. CLUB
Louisiana State Museum Jazz Collection
1978.118(B).07732

110 DUKES AND DUCHESS OF DIXIELAND
Louisiana State Museum Jazz Collection
1978.118(B).02710

111 LOUIS PRIMA
Thomas L. Morgan Collection

112 THE KID ORY BAND AT BEVERLY CAVERN
Louisiana State Museum Jazz Collection
1996.104.7

113 BILL RUSSELL AT A SECOND LINE PARADE
Louisiana State Museum Jazz Collection
1978.118(B).06325

114 SAMMY PENN DRUMMING
Louisiana State Museum Jazz Collection
1978.118(B).05735b

115 BONANO AT THE NEW ORLEANS JAZZ MUSEUM
Louisiana State Museum Jazz Collection
1978.118(B).0850

116 THE AVERY "KID" HOWARD AND GEORGE LEWIS BAND
Louisiana State Museum Jazz Collection
1978.118(B).03825

117 FATS PICHON
Thomas L. Morgan Collection

118 ERNIE CAGNOLATTI AND SAM DUTREY, JR., WITH LAWRENCE MARRERO'S BAND
Louisiana State Museum Jazz Collection
1978.118(B).02823

119 ORANGE KELLIN
Thomas L. Morgan Collection

120 PETE FOUNTAIN, JR., AND WOMEN ON JAZZ DAY, 1959
Louisiana State Museum Jazz Collection
1978.118(B).03160

121 EDMOND HALL
Louisiana State Museum Jazz Collection
1978.118(B).07763d

122 BILLIE PIERCE AND EMANUEL "MANNY" SAYLES
Louisiana State Museum Jazz Collection
1978.118(B).05800

123 THE DUKES OF DIXIELAND
Louisiana State Museum Jazz Collection
T0008.1993.0094

124 LOUIS ARMSTRONG'S CHILDHOOD HOME
Louisiana State Museum Jazz Collection
1978.118(B).00933

126 NEW ORLEANS JAZZ MUSEUM DEDICATION
Louisiana State Museum Jazz Collection
1978.118(B).07754

127 SWEET EMMA BARRETT AND HER JAZZ BAND PLAYING FOR THE KREWE OF WRECKS
Louisiana State Museum Jazz Collection
1978.118(B).02837a-d

128 YOUNG LESLIE MILTON PLAYING DRUMS
Louisiana State Museum Jazz Collection
1978.118(B).05021

129 JOSEPH, ROBICHAUX, AND ANDERSON PLAYING IN CINCINNATI
Louisiana State Museum Jazz Collection
1978.118(B).04244

130 GEORGE "POPS" FOSTER
Louisiana State Museum Jazz Collection
1978.118(B).03118

131 JOHN CASIMIR AT THE MERRY-G-ROUND CLUB
Louisiana State Museum Jazz Collection
1978.118(B).02165

132 DAVE BARTHOLOMEW
Louisiana State Museum Jazz Collection
1978.118(B).00430

133 IRVING "PINKY" VIDACOVICH'S ORCHESTRA
Louisiana State Museum Jazz Collection
1978.118(B).06901

134 TOMMY SANCTON
Preservation Hall
Used with Permission

135 "SWEET" EMMA BARRETT
Preservation Hall
Used with Permission

136 DOLLY ADAMS
Louisiana State Museum Jazz Collection
1978.118(B).00001

137 CONNEE BOSWELL AND PETE FOUNTAIN
Louisiana State Museum Jazz Collection
1978.118(B).00858

138 HENRY "RED" ALLEN, JR.
Louisiana State Museum Jazz Collection
1978.118(B).00091

139 Dave "Fat Man" Williams
Thomas L. Morgan Collection

140 Blanche Thomas and Louis Cottrell
Louisiana State Museum Jazz Collection
1978.118(B).02427

141 Al "Jumbo" Hirt
Louisiana State Museum Jazz Collection
1978.118(B).03752

142 Albert "Papa" French
Louisiana State Museum Jazz Collection
1994.003.33.037

143 Crawford-Ferguson Night Owls
Louisiana State Museum Jazz Collection
1978.118(B).02482

144 Ellis Marsalis
Bob French Collection
Used with Permission

145 The Ernest "Punch" Miller Band
Louisiana State Museum Jazz Collection
1978.118(B).05002

146 Louis Back in Town with Band Teacher Peter Davis
Louisiana State Museum Jazz Collection
1978.118(B).07709

147 Armstrongs with Armstrong Museum Plaque
Louisiana State Museum Jazz Collection
1978.118(B).00333

148 "Muggsy" Spanier
Louisiana State Museum Jazz Collection
1978.118(B).06603

149 Louis in Last Ten Years
Louisiana State Museum Jazz Collection
1978.118(B).00355

150 Paul Barbarin and Boys Drumming
Louisiana State Museum Jazz Collection
T0008.1993.0138

151 Dede and Billie Pierce
Louisiana State Museum Jazz Collection
1978.118(B).05810

152 The Pierces
Louisiana State Museum Jazz Collection
1978.118(B).05831

153 Foster, St. Cyr, and Hines
Louisiana State Museum Jazz Collection
1978.118(B).03125

154 The Pierces No. 2
Louisiana State Museum Jazz Collection
1985.084.33

155 Louis Cottrell, Jr.
Louisiana State Museum Jazz Collection
1978.118(B).02421

156 Wiggs and Band
Louisiana State Museum Jazz Collection
1978.118(B).07011

157 George Lewis with Preservation Hall Band
Louisiana State Museum Jazz Collection
1978.118(B).04537

158 Performance at Preservation Hall
Louisiana State Museum Jazz Collection
1978.118(B).02446

159 Percy Humphrey
Louisiana State Museum Jazz Collection
1978.118(B).00952

160 "Fats" Houston
Louisiana State Museum Jazz Collection
1978.118(B).03797

161 "Fats" Houston at New Orleans Jazz and Heritage Festival
Louisiana State Museum Jazz Collection
1978.118(B).03801

162 Booker T. Glass
Louisiana State Museum Jazz Collection
1978.118(B).03445

163 Funeral Procession of Adolphe Alexander, Jr.
Louisiana State Museum Jazz Collection
1978.118(B).00059

164 Paul Barbarin No. 2
Louisiana State Museum Jazz Collection
T0008.1993.0142

165 Alcide "Slow Drag" Pavageau with the George Lewis Band
Louisiana State Museum Jazz Collection
1978.118(B).05709

166 Pavageau's Funeral
Louisiana State Museum Jazz Collection
1978.118(B).07777

167 Early Fairview Church Band
Louisiana State Museum Jazz Collection
1998.041.23

168 Alan Jaffe and Larry Borenstein
Louisiana State Museum Jazz Collection
1978.118(B).00061

169 Treme Brass Band
Louisiana State Museum Jazz Collection
1994.119.26

170 Armstrong Ceremony
Louisiana State Museum Jazz Collection
1978.118(B).00406

171 Dixieland Band at the Heart Fund
Louisiana State Museum Jazz Collection
1978.118(B).02445

172 Crawford-Ferguson Night Owls No. 2
Louisiana State Museum Jazz Collection
1978.118(B).02477

173 Half-Fast Walking Club
Louisiana State Museum Jazz Collection
1978.118(B).03182

174 Jeanette Kimball
Louisiana State Museum Jazz Collection
1978.118(B).04284

175 Thomas, Alcorn, and Pierson Playing
Louisiana State Museum Jazz Collection
1978.118(B).06790

176 Edward "Montudie" Garland
Louisiana State Museum Jazz Collection
1978.118(B).03348

177 Placide Adams
Louisiana State Museum Jazz Collection
T0008.1993.0003

178 Louis Barbarin
Louisiana State Museum Jazz Collection
T0008.1993.0130a-c

179 ONWARD BRASS BAND
Louisiana State Museum Jazz
Collection
T0008.1993.0132

180 MILTON BATISTE
Louisiana State Museum Jazz
Collection
1978.118(B).02592

**182 STATUE OF LOUIS
ARMSTRONG**
Louisiana State Museum Jazz
Collection
1978.118(B).07296a

**183 DANNY BARKER
PLAYING BANJO**
Louisiana State Museum Jazz
Collection
T0008.1993.0175

184 NEVILLE BROTHERS
Louisiana State Museum Jazz
Collection
1994.003.33.094

185 ALONZO STEWART
Louisiana State Museum Jazz
Collection
1987.070.7

**186 NICHOLAS PAYTON AND
DOC CHEATHAM**
Dick Waterman Collection
Used with Permission

**187 WYNTON AND
BRANFORD MARSALIS**
Louisiana State Museum Jazz
Collection
1994.003.33.040

**188 DANNY AND BLUE LU
BARKER**
Louisiana State Museum Jazz
Collection
1994.003.33.132

**189 THE DIRTY DOZEN
BRASS BAND**
Louisiana State Museum Jazz
Collection
1994.003.33.045

**190 THE ORIGINAL NEW
ORLEANS BUCK
JUMPERS' SECOND LINE**
Louisiana State Museum Jazz
Collection
1994.003.33.151

**191 THE NEW ORLEANS
RAGTIME ORCHESTRA**
Lars Edegran Collection
Used with Permission

192 GERMAINE BAZZLE
Erika Goldring Collection
Used with Permission

**193 PUD BROWN AND
LIONEL FERBOS**
Louisiana State Museum Jazz
Collection
1994.003.33.046

194 DONALD HARRISON
Erika Goldring Collection
Used with Permission

195 ALLEN TOUSSAINT
Dick Waterman Collection
Used with Permission

196 JAMES SINGLETON
Erika Goldring Collection
Used with Permission

197 BANU GIBSON
Dick Waterman Collection
Used with Permission

198 HAROLD BATTISTE
Louisiana State Museum Jazz
Collection
1994.003.33.124

**199 EDWARD "KIDD"
JORDAN**
Erika Goldring Collection
Used with Permission

200 KERMIT RUFFINS
Erika Goldring Collection
Used with Permission